# GAINSBOROUGH & REYNOLDS

*Contrasts in Royal Patronage*

# GAINSBOROUGH & REYNOLDS

*Contrasts*
*in Royal Patronage*

*The Queen's Gallery, Buckingham Palace*

# Contents

© 1994, Her Majesty Queen Elizabeth II

ISBN 1 85894 006 0

All rights reserved

Produced by Merrell Holberton
Designed by Roger Davies
Typeset by August Filmsetting
Printed and bound in Italy by Graphicom

Front cover illustration: detail of No. 16
Back cover illustration: detail of No. 66
Half-title illustration: detail of No. 23
Frontispiece: detail of No. 11

# Introduction

The careers of the two leading painters in Britain during the eighteenth century – Thomas Gainsborough and Sir Joshua Reynolds – form a striking contrast. The differences perhaps stem from aspects of character and personality, but they also incorporate such issues as artistic outlook and practice. Like many other famous figures of the eighteenth century – Samuel Johnson (Nos. 25, 28), James Boswell, Oliver Goldsmith (No. 26), Edmund Burke, Adam Smith, Charles Burney, R.B. Sheridan – both painters were born in the regions but settled in London. Reynolds was quick to appreciate the significance of London, whereas Gainsborough met with his first real success in Bath (in essence a social oupost of London) before finally deciding to live in the metropolis.

The foundation of the Royal Academy in 1768 under the patronage of George III provides one of the clearest illustrations of the separate ways in which Gainsborough and Reynolds approached their art. The appointment of Reynolds as the first President of the Royal Academy was not only an indication of his personal status as an artist, but it also gave him a platform for enunciating his theories about art and his concern to establish the Grand Style. The *Discourses* (Nos. 49, 50), which began as lectures given to the students annually on the anniversary of the Royal Academy's foundation (from 1773 given biennially), amounted at that date to the most significant and sustained text of art criticism ever published in Britain. The delivery of these lectures was not just a matter of intellectual consequence, it was also a social event.

By contrast, although Gainsborough was a founder member of the Royal Academy and exhibited there on several occasions, his relations with the institution were never easy. Indeed, he quarrelled with the Royal Academy in 1773 and 1784, after which he never exhibited there again, preferring to organize his own exhibitions in Schomberg House, his private house in Pall Mall.

The two artists also had very different relationships with the court of George III. Yet, it is to the eternal credit of George IV* that he admired both painters in equal measure. It is these matters that this exhibition addresses.

---

*For the sake of simplicity George IV is referred to throughout this publication as King, although he was of course first Prince of Wales and then from 1811 Prince Regent. He acceded to the throne in 1820 and died in 1830.

# Parallel lives

The lives of Gainsborough and Reynolds serve as a commentary upon one another. Reynolds (fig. 1) was born in 1723 in Plympton in Devon, the son of a schoolmaster. He apparently never completely lost his Devonian accent, which, together with his poor delivery exacerbated by encroaching deafness, always made the *Discourses* difficult to follow. At the age of seventeen Reynolds left Devon for London where he was apprenticed to the portrait painter Thomas Hudson, who, significantly, had in turn been the pupil of Jonathan Richardson the Elder, the author of the only important body of art criticism (*An Essay on the Theory of Painting*, 1715, and *Two Discourses on the Art of Criticism*, 1719) before Reynolds's own *Discourses*. Richardson wrote of the art of portraiture in a way that clearly anticipates Reynolds's theories and circumstances. For example, "A portrait-painter must understand mankind, and enter into their characters, and express their minds as well as their faces: and as his business is chiefly with people of condition, he must think as a gentleman, and a man of sense, or it will be impossible to give such their true, and proper resemblances." Hudson, too, was not simply a successful portrait painter. He had a good library and was an important collector of old master drawings. The youthful, rather scholarly Reynolds may well have been determined to emulate his master.

A chance meeting in Plymouth in 1749 with Commodore (later Admiral) Augustus Keppel (No. 35) resulted in Reynolds sailing to Italy where he spent three and a half years (1749–52), mostly in Rome, but also travelling to Naples, Florence, Bologna, Parma, Mantua, Ferrara, Venice, Milan and Turin. This exposure to Italian art, particularly the work of High Renaissance and seventeenth-century painters, deeply affected Reynolds's ideas about art, which are reflected in his portraits and narrative paintings, as well as in the *Discourses*.

Reynolds now set about becoming a successful portrait painter, establishing himself in London first at an address in St Martin's Lane, then in Great Newport Street in 1753, and finally in 1760 at a house in Leicester Fields (now Leicester Square). He was to remain living at this address as a bachelor for the rest of his life, with his younger sister, Frances, as housekeeper, followed in this capacity by his niece, Mary Palmer, later Marchioness of Thomond. The artist worked hard to gain his reputation and this he did during the mid-1750s and early 1760s as a result of immense productivity, rigorous organization, the dissemination of his compositions through prints, an innovative approach to portraiture, and a tendency to cultivate his social position. Reynolds's pupil, James Northcote, remarked that "Sir Joshua was always cautious to preserve an unblemished character, and careful not to make any man his enemy". The artist's studio was at the house in Leicester Fields, but it was here also that he threw elegant dinner parties and employed liveried footmen. It was from here, too, that he frequently drove out in his ornately decorated coach. In 1772 he had a villa built at Richmond (see No. 36) to a design by Sir William Chambers as an escape from London. Only rarely, however, did he go abroad following the years in Italy: in 1768 and 1771 he visited Paris for short trips and in 1781 and again in 1785 he travelled in the Low Countries during the summer months. He was essentially an urban figure content to remain in London. His success led to public honour, first when still aged only forty-five as President of the Royal Academy, followed immediately by a knighthood and in 1773 an honorary degree at the University of Oxford (No. 58), and then as Principal Painter to George III in 1784. This rise in status is reflected in the remarkably revealing series of self-portraits (No. 66) painted at regular intervals throughout his life, which are comparable only with Rembrandt's concern for his own image.

Reynolds was essentially an autodidact and he enjoyed himself most in the company of writers and intellectuals. He was the prime mover in the foundation of the Literary Club in 1764. Johnson (Nos. 25, 28), Boswell, Edward Gibbon, Goldsmith (No. 26), Charles James Fox, Joseph Banks, Sir William Hamilton, Sheridan, Burke, David Garrick (No. 5) and Reynolds's future biographer, Edmond Malone (see No. 51), were amongst the membership. This was the background against which the *Discourses* were written. Johnson and Burke were

Fig. 1 Sir Joshua Reynolds: *Self-portrait*, 1753–54, oil on canvas, 64.5 × 74.3 cm, National Portrait Gallery, London

deeply influential when it came to discussing the ideas that Reynolds wanted to expound. The *Discourses* (Nos. 49, 50) are central to an understanding of eighteenth-century British art just as they are to an appreciation of Reynolds's own art. The painter says in his last Discourse (XV), "I had seen much, and I had thought much upon what I had seen; I had something of an habit of investigation, and a disposition to reduce all that I observed and felt in my own mind, to method and system . . .". Reynolds was keen not only to elevate the practice and appreciation of painting on to a higher level, but also to raise its status, as Johnson did for the English language with the publication of his *Dictionary* (1755), Garrick did for the theatre, Boswell did for biography, and Burney for music.

For Reynolds the Grand Style had an intellectual basis. "The Art which we profess has beauty for its object; this it is our business to discover and to express; the beauty of which we are in quest is general and intellectual; it is an idea that subsists only in the mind; the sight never beheld it, nor has the hand expressed it: it is an idea residing in the heart of the artist, which he is always labouring to impart, and which he dies at last without imparting, but which he is yet so far able to communicate as to raise the thoughts, and extend the views of the spectator." This process, Reynolds contends, gradually purifies the mind and leads "the thoughts through successive stages of excellence, till that contemplation of universal rectitude and harmony which began by Taste, may, as it is exalted and refined, conclude in Virtue" (Ninth Discourse). The touchstone for the artist hoping to achieve such an

end is the imitation of the art of the past, particularly antiquity and the High Renaissance in so far as those periods set standards of excellence. The 'borrowings' were not to be slavish, and recognisable only to the extent that the practice resulted in the release of imagination in artist and viewer alike. The poses adopted in portraits of men and women undertaken by Reynolds, therefore, evoke the past and thus achieve both grandiloquence and revelation. By this means the character of his sitters, beyond mere likeness, was not suggested by particular or literal details, but by reference to the archetypal. The skill lay in the selection of 'types' to match the respective sitters. Honour was done to the sitter by the range and profundity of the painter's art. Reynolds applied these principles successfully in his portraits of a whole cross-section of society, but in his history and narrative paintings he seems sometimes to have overreached himself. Ironically, it was the application of his ideas in the sphere of history painting that he particularly sought and would have most welcomed. Furthermore, it was not long before younger generations determined to debunk such grand ideas. The artists William Blake, James Barry and John Ruskin, the critic William Haz-

litt, and later the Pre-Raphaelites were dismissive. To a certain extent, this led to a decline in Reynolds's reputation that has only recently begun to be reversed.

Reynolds could easily be thought of as being too cerebral or simply as conceited and calculating. He was undoubtedly conscious of his position and sought to maintain it, but this perhaps stemmed more from his sense of mission than from his personality. It is significant that the elaborate caricatures that he painted in his early years were not repeated at later stages of his life. His circle of friends was wider than might be expected and included leading actresses of the day, as well as raffish characters such as Boswell, John Wilkes and the fencing master Domenico Angelo at whose wild parties the transvestite Chevalier d'Eon (fig. 2) was to be seen. As Fanny Burney wrote, Reynolds was "gay though contemplative, and flew from indolence, though he courted enjoyment". It was Gainsborough who remarked of Reynolds, "Damn him, how various he is", and it was Dr Johnson who said, "Sir, I know of no man who has passed through life with more observation than Reynolds". The ill-fated artist Benjamin Robert Haydon summarised Reynolds's skills as a painter not as "grandeur, or expression, or form, but delicacy of character, elegance of air, harmony of colour".

Clearly Reynolds owed his success as a painter in part to his social skills. He was at ease in society even though he was afflicted late in life by deafness and, in addition, towards the end, by blindness. As a man he was always genial, urbane, self-contained, yet eminently clubbable. At the same time he was genuinely kind, readily concerned for his fellow artists, always encouraging to the young, and permanently generous in spirit to all. There are few scenes as touching as Reynolds answering the summons of his former rival to visit Schomberg House as Gainsborough lay dying during the summer of 1788. Likewise, in spite of certain reservations, Reynolds extolled the virtues of Gainsborough to the students of the Royal Academy in Discourse XIV delivered in the same year as the artist's death. "If ever this nation should produce genius sufficient to acquire to us the honourable distinction of an English School, the name of Gainsborough will be transmitted to posterity, in the history of the Art, among the very first of that rising name."

No contrast between these two artists could be greater than their burials. Gainsborough was buried in Kew churchyard in a simple grave. The pall-bearers were all fellow artists including Reynolds. On the other hand, in 1792 when the first President of the Royal Academy died his body lay in state overnight in Somerset House. There was an elaborate funeral service in St Paul's Cathedral where he was buried in the crypt and where the sculptor John Flaxman several years later carved a statue that was erected in the nave. The pall-bearers were his aristocratic friends — three dukes, two marquises, three earls and one baron — and the congregation included leading members of British cultural life. This was perhaps a fitting conclusion to the life of a man who had sought to give a specific identity to a national school of art, or, as Burke phrased it, "He was the first Englishman who added the praise of the elegant Arts to the other glories of his Country".

Gainsborough (fig. 3) was born in 1727 in Sudbury in Suffolk. He was the son of a clothier, who at one stage ran a shroud-making firm and made crêpe for funerals. The artist's talent emerged early while he was still at school and ca. 1740 he was duly sent

Fig. 3 Thomas Gainsborough: *Self-portrait*, ca. 1759, oil on canvas, 76.2 × 63.5 cm, National Portrait Gallery, London

to London to serve an apprenticeship with the French engraver and draughtsman Hubert François Gravelot. With Gravelot Gainsborough learnt about aspects of design in the context of the applied arts. He also became subject to the influence of French art through seeing works by Watteau, Mercier and Jean-Baptiste Van Loo. Later these terms of reference widened to include Boucher, Fragonard, Perronneau and Maurice-Quentin de La Tour. The initial impact of French art on Gainsborough was not forgotten and lingered in his work, being most evident in the underlying sense of Rococo design and an open-minded approach to the use of materials including chalks and pastels.

Of British artists, William Hogarth and Francis Hayman seem to have held Gainsborough's attention, especially as regards the development of the conversation piece and the fluent handling of paint. Alongside these influences, which encouraged Gainsborough in the painting of portraits, the importation of Dutch pictures helped him to realise his potential for the art of landscape. The advantage of seeing works by Jacob Ruisdael, Jan Wynants, Jan Both and Philip Wouwermans is reflected in many of

Gainsborough's early landscapes. By the mid-1740s he had established a studio in Hatton Gardens and immediately married Margaret Burr – she was probably already pregnant – by whom the painter later had two surviving daughters (Mary and Margaret) who were to be immortalised in paint by their father on many occasions. The early years in London reveal that Gainsborough was of an independent mind: he studied the kind of art that appealed to him and he was not interested in precepts. His feeling for nature was so strong that it was in danger of being expunged if he allowed himself to become too exposed to academic discipline.

The artist's innate instinct for composition and freedom of spirit becomes most apparent after he returned to Suffolk in 1748. He set up a studio at first in Sudbury and then in 1752 in Ipswich. Famous portraits like *Mr and Mrs Robert Andrews* (National Gallery, London) or *Heneage Lloyd and his Sister, Lucy* (Fitzwilliam Museum, Cambridge) illustrate Gainsborough's ability to capture the natural disposition of his sitters and to blend them in with their rural surroundings. Yet, however admired the paintings of these years are now, they did not increase the artist's reputation significantly during his lifetime. After a short tour of the Midlands as an itinerant painter in 1758–59 he suddenly moved to Bath where he lived for fifteen years and from 1766 in a house on The Circus. This was the turning point in his life. Not only did he find numerous sitters for his portraits, but he had easy access to the countryside. His art flourished and his output increased. From 1761 he sent paintings for exhibition in London at the Society of Artists and from 1769 he contributed intermittently to the exhibitions at the newly founded Royal Academy of Arts. It was in Bath that the true personality of the artist emerged.

Gainsborough's character was diametrically opposed to that of Reynolds. He was mercurial, capricious and quixotic. He was obviously of a nervous disposition, tending to fall ill from exhaustion. The style of his letters – disorganized, teeming with observations, flashes of humour, rambling, ribald, idiosyncratically punctuated – is the essence of the man, who seems, in contrast with Reynolds, rarely to have indulged in self-portraiture. He once wrote to a friend, William Jackson, "I am the most inconsistent, changeable being, so full of fits and starts, that if

you mind what I say, it will be shutting your Eyes to some purpose". It is clear that he set out to enjoy life and that, although painting was in some respects a celebration of life, it was also a laborious and tedious form of income. One of his daughters told the diarist Joseph Farington that "her father often exceeded the bounds of temperance and his Health suffered from it, being occasionally unable to work for a week afterwards ... He often wondered at Reynolds' *equal* application". Reynolds himself declared that Gainsborough "had a painter's eye, but not a painter's mind". In truth, Gainsborough's proclivity was for music (he played the viola da gamba) and his close friends wherever he lived were musicians – amateurs like William Jackson, William Wollaston, Philip and Anne Thicknesse, as well as celebrated players like J.C. Bach, Felice de' Giardini and Carl Friedrich Abel. Jackson states that "Gainsborough's profession was painting, music was his amusement. Yet there were times when music seemed to be his employment, and painting his diversion". But, "though possessed of ear, taste, and genius, he never had application enough to learn his notes". Jackson concludes, "His conversation was sprightly, but licentious; his favourite subjects were music and painting, which he treated in a manner peculiarly his own; the common topics, or any of a superior cast, he thoroughly hated, and always interrupted by some stroke of wit or humour".

Unlike Reynolds, therefore, Gainsborough did not court the company of literary men and only occasionally read a book. It is not difficult to imagine how he needed little encouragement to leave his studio as he grew tired of portraiture. Gainsborough once wrote to Jackson that what he dearly wanted was "to take my Viol da Gamba and walk off to some sweet village where I can paint Landskips and enjoy the fag End of Life in quietness and ease ... But we can say nothing of these things you know Jackson, we must jogg on and be content with the jingling of the Bells, only damn it I hate a dust, the Kicking up of a dust, and being confined *in Harness* to follow the track, while others ride in the waggon, undercover, stretching their Legs in the straw *at Ease*, and gazing at Green Trees & Blue skies, without half my *Taste*, that's damned hard". The demands of portrait painting were such that Gainsborough could be cynical about his intentions.

He writes to Jackson on 21 September 1767, "Damn Gentlemen, there is not such a set of Enemies to a real artist in the world as they are, if not kept at a proper distance. *They* think (and so may you for a while) that they reward your merit by their company and notice; but I who blow away all the chaff & by G___ in their eyes too if they don't stand clear, know that they have but one part worth looking at, and that is their Purse...". There is an echo of this letter in one addressed to Sir William Chambers in 1783: "...you know my cunning way of avoiding great subjects in painting & of concealing my ignorance by a flash in the pan. If I can do this while I pick pockets in the portrait way two or three years longer I intend to turn into a cot & turn into a serious fellow...".

The tone of Gainsborough's letters can be deceptive and he did formulate specific ideas about painting that he defended quite zealously on occasions. These theories were not in line with those expounded by Reynolds in the *Discourses* and, to a certain extent, they anticipate later developments in British painting. Gainsborough, for instance, was firmly against purely topographical landscape as he rather tartly pointed out to the Earl of Hardwicke (ca. 1762–63): "Mr Gainsborough presents his Humble respects to Lord Hardwicke and shall always think it an honor to be employ'd in anything for his Lordship; but with respect to *real Views* from Nature in this country he has never seen any Place that affords a Subject equally to the poorest imitations of Gaspar or Claude... Mr. G. hopes Lord Hardwicke will not mistake his meaning, but if his Lordship wishes to have anything tolerable of the name of G., the subject altogether, as well as figures etc., must be of his own Brain, otherwise Lord Hardwicke will only pay for Encouraging a Man out of his way and had much better buy a picture of some of the good Old Masters." His landscapes, therefore, were to be the product of a creative imagination, but were to be no less atmospheric as a result of his method of composition. As Constable wrote of Gainsborough, "His object was to deliver a fine sentiment, the depths of twilight, and the dews and pearls of the morning, are all to be found on the canvases of this most benevolent and kindhearted man. On looking at them, we find tears in our eyes, & know not what brings them".

It was the same with portraiture, where the question of modern dress, as opposed to the timeless quality of garments suggestive of antiquity, was a relevant issue in terms of both the contemporary portrait and history painting. Gainsborough was certain that modern dress enhanced a likeness and in no doubt that it heightened characterization. As he wrote firmly to the Earl of Dartmouth in 1771, "My Lord I am very well aware of the Objection to modern dresses in Pictures that they are soon out of fashion and look awkward, but as that misfortune cannot be helped we must set it against the unluckiness of fancied dresses taking away Likenesses, the principal beauty and intention of a Portrait".

Gainsborough evidently considered such problems as and when they arose. Indeed, the need for such explanations seems to have arisen as he grew to be more successful. Bath was where Gainsborough's art grew to maturity. He began to paint on a larger scale and his compositions, both as regards portraiture and landscapes, became more dramatic. This may partly have been because his terms of reference suddenly widened. Gainsborough never travelled abroad, but success gave him access to famous collections of art in the south of England that provided examples of the European tradition that he was heir to, and included works by artists that were to be important for his subsequent development, particularly Van Dyck for portraiture and Rubens for landscape. Throughout his life Gainsborough made copies after earlier artists (No. 48), but he copied no artist more than Van Dyck. Occasionally, as in *The harvest waggon* of 1767 (The Barber Institute of Fine Arts, Birmingham) or in *Diana and Actaeon* (No. 15), Gainsborough clearly does quote from other artists, but, on the whole, this was not his usual method of working.

The exercising of the artist's imagination on the strength of his own observation fuelled by examination of works by the old masters is perhaps best revealed in Gainsborough's so called 'fancy pictures' combining aspects of portraiture, landscape, and poetry. These paintings have an arcadian flavour even when confronting social issues, and were immensely popular in their time. Reynolds also painted such subjects, but, as with Gainsborough, they soon fell out of fashion, owing to what appeared to be a pronounced sentimentality. Significantly, Reynolds bought Gainsborough's *The girl with pigs* (The Hon. Simon Howard, Castle Howard) when it was exhibited at the Royal Academy in 1782. On hearing this, Gainsborough replied, "I think myself highly honor'd and much obliged to you for this mark of your favour: I may truly say, I have bought my Piggs to a fine market". *Diana and Actaeon* (No. 15) is related to the 'fancy pictures', but cannot be categorized as such. It does, nonetheless, indicate that even at the very end of his life Gainsborough continued to explore new themes and to accept new challenges.

A singular aspect of Gainsborough's art was his unusual working methods. For his conversation pieces even at an early date he used lay-figures. He had a fascination for the artificial lighting effects created by the use of transparencies with candles found in 'peepshows' and theatrical spectacles. Gainsborough's own 'peepshow' box for which he painted transparencies is in the Victoria and Albert Museum. Several sources (including Reynolds in Discourse XIV) refer to Gainsborough's methods of 'composing' his landscapes in his studio using an array of props. "He would place cork or coal for his foregrounds; make middle grounds of sand or clay, bushes of mosses and lichens, and set up distant woods of broccoli."

Similar unorthodoxies are apparent in Gainsborough's actual technique of painting, particularly during his later years. For the laying in of the forms he worked in a darkened studio usually by candlelight. More light was admitted for finishing portraits or landscapes, at which stage he would add translucent glazes to render the evanescent effects of light as accurately as possible. The low light levels, however, probably account for the bright flesh tones that are so characteristic of the artist. Usually he stood while painting, sometimes with brushes of extended length (a full six feet), placing himself at right angles to the sitter so that "he touched the features of his picture exactly at the same distance at which he viewed the sitter". The canvas was often loosened from the stretcher so that it could be more easily moved. Portraits were always done from life. Gainsborough's pictures always have the appearance of being painted very fast, in much the same way as his drawings are immensely broad in style and spirited in touch. Reynolds, for instance, observed that instead of painting the image in parts, Gainsborough had the "manner of forming all the parts of his picture together; the whole going on at the same time, in the same manner as Nature creates her works". Yet Reynolds was puzzled by this dazzling technique, although he understood the effect that Gainsborough was seeking. He told the students at the Royal Academy, "It is certain that all those odd scribbles and marks, which, on a close examination, are so observable in Gainsborough's pictures, and which even to experienced painters appear rather the effect of accident than design: this chaos, this uncouth and shapeless appearance, by a kind of magic, at a certain distance assumes form, and all the parts seem to drop into their proper places, so that we can hardly refuse acknowledging the full effect of diligence, under the appearance of chance and hasty negligence."

In view of his unusual working methods it is hardly surprising that Gainsborough felt strongly about how his pictures should be displayed. If such matters were left to others the visual subtleties could well be lost. As Reynolds said, Gainsborough required his pictures to be "seen near, as well as at a distance". Matters came to a head on two occasions at the Royal Academy. In 1772 Gainsborough had written to Garrick giving the actor advice on how a portrait should be hung in his own house. "A Word to the Wise; if you let your Portrait hang up so high, only consult your Room, and to insinnuate something over the other Door, it never can look without a hardness of Countenance and the Painting flat, it was calculated for breast high and will never have its Effect of likeness otherwise". The following year Gainsborough wrote to Garrick to say that he would not be submitting any pictures: "I don't send to the Exhibition this year; they hang my likenesses too high to be seen, & have refused to lower one sail to oblige me".

This was not to be the only such incident concerning the activities of the Hanging Committee of the Royal Academy. In 1782 Gainsborough painted a set of ovals of George III and Queen Charlotte and their thirteen children (No. 23) and these were shown at the Royal Academy in 1783. Having carefully established the order in which the ovals should be hung "with the Frames touching each other, in this order", he then had to issue a further warning.

Fig. 4 Thomas Gainsborough: *Anne, Duchess of Cumberland,* 1777, oil on canvas, 238.1 × 142.2 cm, The Royal Collection

Fig. 5 Thomas Gainsborough: *Henry, Duke of Cumberland,* 1777, oil on canvas, 238.1 × 142.2 cm, The Royal Collection

"Mr. Gainsborough presents his Compliments to the Gentlemen appointed to hang the Pictures at the Royal Academy; and begs leave to *hint* to Them, that if The Royal Family, which he has sent for this Exhibition, (*being smaller than three quarters*) are hung above the line along with full lengths, he never more, whilst he breathes, will send another Picture to the Exhibition – This he swears to God." Finally, in 1784, Gainsborough broke with the Royal Academy irrevocably, this time over the hanging of *The Three Eldest Princesses* (No. 9). The Committee warned Gainsborough that they would not make an exception and hang this picture below the accepted height for full-lengths. Gainsborough insisted: "Mr. Gainsborough's Comp.ts to the Gent.n of the Com-

mittee, & begs pardon for giving them so much trouble; but as he has painted this Picture of the Princesses in so tender a light, that notwithstanding he approves very much of the established Line for Strong Effects, he cannot possibly consent to have it placed higher than five feet & a half, because the likenesse & Work of the Picture will not be seen any higher; therefore at a Word, he will not trouble the Gentlemen against their Inclination, but will beg the rest of his Pictures back again." Gainsborough never sent another picture for exhibition at the Royal Academy.

By this stage of his career, however, Gainsborough did not need to rely on exhibiting his paintings at the Academy. His years in Bath had proved to be rewarding, although his sudden departure in 1774 may have been caused by a shortage of commissions. This would certainly not be the case in London and Gainsborough clearly had sufficient funds to take a tenancy on the west wing of Schomberg House in Pall Mall where he was to live for the rest of his life. The house was owned by an artist, John Astley, who had married a rich widow and lived in the centre part. The east wing was leased to a Dr Graham, a purveyor of quack remedies involving a Temple of Health and a Celestial Bed on which naked bodies were encouraged to sprawl. Gainsborough's studio was in an extension added to the south side of the house overlooking the gardens of Marlborough House. It was here that he organized his own exhibitions after his disagreement with the Royal Academy. Although Gainsborough's wife did not like to spend money, the artist did at this late stage in his life acquire a coach, invest in goverment stock and buy a country house at Richmond (close to the one owned by Reynolds) as well as a cottage on Sir Henry Bate-Dudley's estate in Essex. He also bought old masters in the sale room at Christie's, whose premises were at that time nearby in Pall Mall.

Regardless of his difficulties with the Royal Academy, Gainsborough was in great demand as a portrait painter. This was partly because he had now secured royal patronage, announcing this to the world by exhibiting full-length portraits of the Duke and Duchess of Cumberland (figs. 4, 5) at the Royal Academy on his return after a four-year gap to the annual exhibitions in 1777. The pictures he submitted to the exhibitions in 1777 and 1778 included some of his greatest portraits: *The Hon. Mrs Thomas Graham* (National Gallery of Scotland, Edinburgh) and *Carl Friedrich Abel* (Henry E. Huntington Library and Art Gallery, San Marino), both exhibited in 1777, and *Mrs John Elliott* (Metropolitan Museum, New York), exhibited in 1778. During the 1780s the number of royal commissions increased steadily. Gainsborough also now painted landscapes of great distinction. *The watering place* (National Gallery, London), which was exhibited in 1777, was described by Horace Walpole as "by far the finest landscape ever painted in England, & equal to the great Masters". Further travel to the West Country (ca. 1782) and the Lake District (1783) increased the

possibilities as far as landscape was concerned, but these important late landscapes did not always sell. The artist Sir William Beechey remarked that in Schomberg House such pictures "stood ranged in long lines from his hall to his painting-room, and they who came to sit for him for their portraits, for which he was chiefly employed, rarely deigned to honor them with a look as they passed them".

It was from Schomberg House that Gainsborough wrote his moving letter inviting Reynolds to come and see him towards the end of July 1788:

Dear Sir Joshua, I am just to write what I fear you will not read — after lying in a dying state for 6 months. The extreme affection which I am informed of by a Friend which Sir Joshua has expressed induces me to beg a last favour, which is to come once under my Roof and look at my things, my woodman you never saw, if what I ask now is not disagreeable to your feeling that I may have the honour to speak to you. I can from a sincere Heart say that I always admired and sincerely loved Sir Joshua Reynolds.

Tho. Gainsborough.

Reynolds records his somewhat ambivalent reactions in his Discourse XIV. "I am aware how flattering it is to myself to be thus connected with the dying testimony which this excellent painter bore to his art. But I cannot prevail on myself to suppress, that I was not connected with him, by any habits of familiarity; if any little jealousies had subsisted between us, they were forgotten, in those moments of sincerity; and he turned towards me as one, who was engrossed by the same pursuits, and who deserved his good opinion, by being sensible of his excellence. Without entering into a detail of what passed at this last interview, the impression of it upon my mind was, that his regret at losing life, was principally the regret of leaving his art; and more especially as he now began, he said, to see what his deficiencies were; which, he said, he flattered himself in his last works were in some measure supplied."

Thus were these two remarkable British painters reconciled.

The foundation of the Royal Academy in 1768 under the patronage of George III provided a forum for the visual arts in Britain. Such a forum was necessary because during the first half of the eighteenth century artists had been divided by factionalism. Academies had been formed in London by Sir Godfrey Kneller (St Luke's) and William Hogarth (St Martin's) for the purposes of tuition, but what was really needed was a space in which to hold exhibitions. An approach was made in 1753–55 by the St Martin's Academy to the Society of Dilettanti formed during the 1730s, but this foundered and an alliance was made in 1759–60 with the Society of Arts (Society for the Encouragement of Arts, Manufactures and Commerce). This proved to be beneficial for the mounting of exhibitions. A rival institution, the Society of Artists of Great Britain, also began to hold exhibitions in Spring Gardens. Artists like Reynolds and Gainsborough were forced to choose between these two groups. Discussions caused further fragmentation: the Society of Arts evolved into the Free Society of Artists and the Society of Artists became the Incorporated Society of Artists.

From such divisions ideas for a proper Academy emerged. The architect William Chambers (No. 56), who taught architecture and architectural drawing to George III, drew the King's attention to the fact that "many artists of reputation ... were very desirous of establishing a society that should more effectively promote the arts of design than any other established, but they were sensible that their design could not be carried into execution without his majesty's patronage". Once royal patronage was forthcoming the idea of a new academy on a formal footing quickly developed. Chambers had proved to be instrumental in the negotiations, but after a certain amount of hesitation Reynolds emerged as the first elected President. He was to prove to be the ideal man for the task by virtue of his standing as a painter, his acceptance by society, his desire to promote the status of art, and his concern for the students. The *Discourses* was the first published text that addressed issues pertinent to the formation of painters and set out principles for them to follow.

The constitution of the Royal Academy allowed for forty full members, some of whom held specific offices (Keeper, Treasurer, Secretary). Those elected as academicians represented a good cross-section of artists: painters, engravers, watercolourists, sculptors, miniaturists, architects. Zoffany, who painted *The Academicians of the Royal Academy* (No. 57) ca. 1771, was proposed personally by George III. Two female academicians were admitted (Mary Moser and Angelica Kauffmann) – a situation that was not repeated until the 1920s. Four professors were appointed – Edward Penny for Painting, Thomas Sandby for Architecture, Samuel Wale for Perspective, and Dr William Hunter for Anatomy. In addition, from 1770, certain honorary members were invited to take up specific posts (Professor of Ancient History, Professor of Ancient Literature, Secretary for Foreign Correspondence). In the first instance these were mainly friends of the President – Johnson (Nos. 25, 28), Goldsmith (No. 26), Giuseppe Baretti (No. 59) and Boswell.

The premises occupied by the Royal Academy were on the south side of Pall Mall towards Trafalgar Square (on the site of the present Institute of Directors), but there was not really sufficient space for all the Academy's activities and so George III made certain rooms available in Old Somerset House (a former royal palace) at the end of the Strand. The move was made in part in 1771, but Chambers was instructed to redesign Old Somerset House for the use of the Royal Academy, the Royal Society and the Society of Antiquaries. This conversion was completed in 1780. The imposing classical façade overlooking the Strand was the principal aspect of the building on the outside, but the main features inside were the long spiral staircase (the subject of a famous drawing by Thomas Rowlandson) and the Great Room. It was here that George III together with members of the Royal Family used to visit the annual exhibitions (Nos. 55, 61). George IV, when Prince of Wales and Prince Regent, surpassed this affiliation by not only visiting the exhibitions but also on occasions attending the annual dinners.

It might be supposed that because of George III's close interest in the burgeoning of the Royal

Fig. 6 Sir Joshua Reynolds: *George III*, 1780, oil on canvas, 236 × 146 cm, Royal Academy of Arts, London

Fig. 7 Sir Joshua Reynolds: *Queen Charlotte*, 1780, oil on canvas, 236 × 146 cm, Royal Academy of Arts, London

Academy he would be on good terms with the first President. In fact, the contrary was the case. According to Northcote, "The King and Queen could not endure the presence of him; he was poison to their sight". On a personal basis, they seem to have found Reynolds cold, aloof and unapproachable. The election to the office of President was followed by a knighthood after which Johnson apparently broke his rule of abstinence (he favoured tea and sherbet) and "drank a glass of wine to the health of Sir Joshua Reynolds". All business concerning the Royal Academy was conducted through Chambers, who Reynolds described as being "Vice-roy over him", and when Lord Eglinton (No. 3) encouraged George III to sit for Reynolds, the King replied trenchantly, "Mr. Ramsay is my painter, my Lord".

Indeed, Ramsay remained Principal Painter until his death in 1784, when Reynolds was duly appointed. This was a post that the President did not enjoy. As he wrote to the Duke of Rutland (24 September 1784), "The place which I have the honour of holding, of the King's principal painter, is a place of not so much profit, and of near equal dignity with His Majesty's rat catcher. The salary is £38 per annum, and for every whole length I am to be paid £50, instead of £200 which I have from everybody else". Beyond personality it is perfectly possible that George III did not like Reynolds for political reasons, since the painter had befriended many of the people who were helping to form radical opinions in the country, quite apart from being friends with those surrounding the Prince of Wales, or those in alliance with the Duchess of Gloucester (No. 18). Also, Reynolds's style did not appeal particularly to the literal-minded George III — classical allusions and allegory were not exactly the most

Fig. 8 Thomas
Gainsborough:
*The Mall*, 1783,
oil on canvas,
120.5 × 146.1 cm, Frick
Collection, New York

direct or winning way of undertaking contemporary portraiture as far as the King was concerned. The concept was too intellectual and grandiose: the Royal Family perhaps felt a little threatened by the awe-inspiring Reynolds, who was perhaps also too courtly. It is hardly surprising, therefore, that Reynolds failed to produce his best work for the court. The portraits of George III and Queen Charlotte painted in 1779 for the Royal Academy are clumsy, awkward and lifeless (no. 62, figs. 6, 7). The portrait of George III when Prince of Wales (No. 7) and the oil-sketch of his marriage ceremony (No. 20) remained in the artist's studio until his death. Neither were the portraits of George III's uncle (William Augustus, Duke of Cumberland) and brother (Edward, Duke of York – No. 2) any more convincing or sympathetic.

However, it was different with Gainsborough, who was described by Northcote as "a natural gentleman". It would seem that the artist was introduced into royal circles by Joshua Kirby, who had taught George III perspective. Kirby had been a lifelong friend of Gainsborough, who asked to be buried next to him in Kew churchyard. His first certain royal commission was for the full-length portraits of the Duke and Duchess of Cumberland (figs. 4, 5) exhibited at the Royal Academy in 1777. As Sir Oliver Millar has written, "The portraits of the vicious little Duke, nervously fingering his George as he steals across the stage, and his raffish Duchess with her lovely eyes, are the most intelligent and amusing of all portraits bounded by the conventions of the state portrait". Soon Gainsborough was, in the words of a contemporary, "quite established at Buckingham House" and had become "the Apollo of the Palace". He was not as difficult to talk to as Reynolds. Indeed, Gainsborough amusingly remarked that he talked "bawdy to the king, & morality to the Prince of Wales". At the Royal Academy exhibition of 1781, Gainsborough included his full-length images of George III (No. 13) and Queen Charlotte (No. 16), which are assuredly the finest such portraits of the reign. This is particularly the case as regards the portrait of Queen Charlotte, which Millar describes as "the most sympathetic portrait painted of the Queen. The sympathy is matched, by Gainsborough's incomparable sensibility and skill, with tenderness, a latent gaity and a magic sense of poetry". These portaits were followed by the series of ovals of the

Fig. 9 Peter Simon after Thomas Gainsborough: *The Woodman*, 1787, stipple engraving (1791), British Museum, London

Royal Family (No. 23) painted in the autumn of 1782 at Windsor Castle and exhibited at the Royal Academy in 1783. This series of ovals was an innovation in royal iconography and a marvellous display of the artist's technique.

George III and Queen Charlotte maintained their interest in Gainsborough. There is some evidence to suggest that George III commissioned a painting entitled *The Richmond Water-walk* ca. 1785 as a pendant to the *The Mall* (New York, Frick Collection) painted in 1783 (fig. 8). For some reason the painting was not finished and may not even have been begun, although several striking studies made in preparation for it have survived. The King was definitely impressed by the *The Woodman*, which is the picture that Gainsborough refers to in his final letter to Reynolds. It was taken to Buckingham House in 1788 for

the King to see, but he did not buy it. The picture was destroyed by fire in 1810 and is only known now from a print (fig. 9). The Queen at some stage acquired the portrait of *Carl Friedrich Abel*, now in the Huntington Library and Art Gallery in San Marino, possibly at the sale in Schomberg House organized by the painter's widow in April and May 1789. At this same sale the Queen almost certainly bought some drawings in coloured chalks by Gainsborough. But the portrait of *Carl Friedrich Abel* and as many as twenty drawings collected by Queen Charlotte were dispersed in her own sale held at Christie's on 24–25 May 1819. Not one example of a drawing in coloured chalks by Gainsborough has been seen in recent years.

Another potential buyer at the studio sale organized by Thomas Gainsborough's widow in April and May 1789 was George IV, who was then still Prince of Wales. He was, however, not in a position to buy anything directly, since the fact that Gainsborough's wife had to sell at all was in part due to the failure of George IV to pay any of his debts. The amount outstanding was £1,228.10s, which was not only a considerable amount but also demonstrates that the Prince of Wales must have been patronising the artist from an early age (his early twenties in fact). The pictures that had been painted by Gainsborough for George IV were listed by the artist's widow (ca. 1792) and include the full-length portrait of the Prince of Wales with a horse now at Waddesdon Manor (see No. 43), which he gave to his friend Colonel St Leger, whose own portrait by Gainsborough (fig. 10) he commissioned and retained: both were exhibited at the Royal Academy in 1782. On the list there were also two portraits of ladies who featured rather prominently in George IV's life, namely *Mrs Fitzherbert* (now Palace of the Legion of Honor, San Francisco) and *Mrs Robinson*, known as 'Perdita' after her role in *The Winter's Tale*. An oil-sketch of Mrs Robinson exists in the Royal Collection, but the finished picture is now in the Wallace Collection having been given by George IV to the Marquess of Hertford in 1818. Two further pictures on the list were late landscapes (*Valley with a shepherd and his flock* in a private collection and *The harvest waggon* now in the Art Gallery of Ontario, Toronto), both of which were given by George IV to Mrs Fitzherbert in 1810.

Some of the paintings left in the artist's studio at his death were subsequently sold either at Mrs Gainsborough's sale (Christie's, 2 June 1792) or at his nephew Gainsborough Dupont's sale (Christie's, 10 April 1797). These sales were further opportunities for George IV to acquire fine works by the artist. The magnificent oval — to a certain extent inspired by Watteau — of *Henry, Duke of Cumberland with the Duchess of Cumberland and Lady Elizabeth Luttrell* (No. 4) was in the former and the separate unfinished studies of the Duke and Duchess of Cumberland (Nos. 1, 22) were in the latter, together with the

*Diana and Actaeon* (No. 15), which is one of the most significant late paintings by Gainsborough from the point of view of style and subject-matter. Another important painting by Gainsborough, the portrait of his son-in-law Johann Christian Fischer (No. 12), which has recently been shown to have been painted over an image of Shakespeare, was given to George IV by one of his younger brothers, Ernest, Duke of Cumberland. Of the paintings that George IV commissioned for himself, the portrait of *Charles, second Earl and first Marquess Cornwallis* (No. 21), dating from ca. 1782, illustrates his incessant search for heroes, whereas the ill-fated canvas of *The Three Eldest Princesses* (No. 9), which was finished in 1784 but cut down at the beginning of Queen Victoria's reign, demonstrates the strength of his affection for his family. This portrait, like Nos. 1 and 22 by Gainsborough, was specially painted for display in Carlton House. It will be recalled that it was the decision to hang this picture so high on the walls of the Royal Academy in 1784 that caused Gainsborough to break irrevocably with that institution.

George IV was a man of enthusiasms and of taste. He admired Reynolds as well as Gainsborough. It was found that on Reynolds's death the Prince of Wales was also in debt to this artist to the amount of £682.10s. The works listed in this connexion included the magnificent full-length portrait of *George IV with a servant*, which was exhibited at the Royal Academy in 1787 and was given to Lord Moira in 1810. It is now in the collection of the Duke of Norfolk (fig. 11). In fact, George IV, unlike his father, was not averse to being painted by Reynolds and he also commissioned or initiated some important full-length portraits from the artist: Frederick, Duke of York (1788) (No. 17), Viscount Keppel (1786), Lord Rodney (1789), and Louis-Philippe, Duke of Chartres (1785), all of which were hung in Carlton House. The portrait of the Duke of Chartres was damaged in a fire at Carlton House in 1824. It was much admired in its day even though the sitter was strongly disliked for his personal behaviour and despised for his conduct towards Louis XVI at the time of the French Revolution. This so upset George IV as well that he took the painting down from view,

Fig. 10 Thomas Gainsborough: *Colonel St Leger*, 1782, oil on canvas, 247.6 × 188 cm, The Royal Collection

although he allowed it on occasions to be studied by artists. The portrait of *David Garrick* (No. 5) was bought by Lord Yarmouth for the Prince Regent at the sale of Edmund Burke's collection held at Christie's on 5 June 1812. Similarly, the late portrait of Lord Moira (No. 37) was painted for Frederick, Duke of York, at whose sale (Christie's, 7 April 1827) George IV acquired it (fig. 12).

Some of the finest paintings by Reynolds owned by George IV were presented to him as gifts. The large paintings of the Marquess of Granby (No. 11) and the Count of Schaumburg-Lippe (No. 6), both dating from the mid-1760s, were given to George IV by Lady Townshend in 1810, and were hung in the Crimson Drawing Room of Carlton House. Lord Rivers gave George IV the equestrian portrait of John, 1st Earl Ligonier dating from 1760, which was duly delivered to Carlton House but was ultimately given to the National Gallery by William IV in 1836 and is now in the Tate Gallery. Lord Erskine (No. 47) made a present of his own portrait in 1810, but it is not absolutely clear how the portraits of Lord Southampton (ca. 1760) (No. 10) and the Earl of Eglinton (1784) (No. 3) came into George IV's possession.

Fig. 11 Sir Joshua Reynolds: *George IV with a servant*, 1787, oil on canvas, 239 × 148 cm, Duke of Norfolk, Arundel Castle

Fig. 12 Sir Joshua Reynolds: *Francis Rawdon-Hastings, 2nd Earl of Moira and 1st Marquess of Hastings*, 1790, oil on canvas, 240 × 147.9 cm, The Royal Collection

Reynolds's niece, Lady Thomond, was particularly generous to George IV, presenting him at intervals with several paintings: the late *Self-portrait* (No. 66) in 1812, *Cymon and Iphigenia* (No. 14) in 1814, *George III when Prince of Wales* (No. 7) in 1815, and *St Michael*, a large copy after Guido Reni that Reynolds had hung from the ceiling of his studio, in 1818. When writing to George IV in connection with the *Self-portrait* (No. 66), Lady Thomond recalled "the kind sentiments your Royal Highness was pleased to express for my late uncle". It is of interest, too, that George IV commissioned the enamellist Henry Bone to copy several of Reynolds's narrative compositions (Nos. 29, 31, 67, 68, 69), which he then displayed in his Private Apartments in Carlton House in their elaborate frames.

Finally, at Lady Thomond's sale (Christie's, 19 May 1821), George IV acquired *The Death of Dido* (No. 8). Both this picture, exhibited in 1781, and *Cymon and Iphigenia* (No. 14), exhibited in 1789, were narrative compositions of a kind that were relatively rare in Reynolds's œuvre. Owing to the artist's technique, however, the condition of these last two paintings has unfortunately deteriorated over the years, but they do bear out a comment made by Gainsborough to the effect that "in his opinion Sir Joshua's pictures in their most decayed state were better than those of any other artists when in their best".

# 1

**Thomas Gainsborough**
*Henry, Duke of*
*Cumberland (1745–1790)*

Oil on canvas, 74.3 × 50.4 cm (the canvas has been considerably reduced in size: the dimensions given in Richard Redgrave's inventory undertaken for Queen Victoria are 127 × 100.5 cm)

Millar 395

*References*: Waterhouse, *Gainsborough*, no. 177

*Notes*: 1. Christie's, 10 April 1797, lot 25.

The sitter was George III's youngest brother. His early life was dissolute, but his marriage in 1771 to Anne Horton (No. 22), although disapproved of by the King, did to some extent improve his moral conduct. The Duke and Duchess of Cumberland were in principle never officially accepted at court. They were often in financial difficulties and spent long periods abroad. In many ways their lifestyle could be described as a formative influence on George IV, who for a time frequented Cumberland House.

Anne Horton was the daughter of Lord Irnham, the head of an old Irish family, described by Lady Louisa Stuart as "the greatest reprobate in England". The marriage to the Duke of Cumberland took place when Anne Horton was aged twenty-seven and already a widow.

The picture was painted towards the end of 1783, together with No. 22, for George IV, who apparently intended to display both portraits in the Saloon at Carlton House. Even though unfinished, the portraits were included, like No. 9, in the exhibition Gainsborough organized in Schomberg House in July 1784 after he had broken with the Royal Academy. The portrait was acquired by George IV at Gainsborough Dupont's sale.[1] The figure was presumably meant to be three-quarters length and to have worn robes of state. Only the head and the immediate surrounding background have been sketched in, and the robes briefly indicated. The form of the figure would next have been laid in, as in No. 22, but for some reason the portrait was abandoned at an early stage.

## 2

**Sir Joshua Reynolds**

*Edward Augustus, Duke of York*
*(1739–1767)*

Oil on canvas, 76.8 × 63.2 cm

Millar 1013

The sitter is depicted wearing the undress uniform of a Flag Officer with the star (half concealed by the lapel) and ribbon of the Order of the Garter. He is seen in profile against a stormy sky. Sittings were given to Reynolds in late 1758 and early 1759, with the uniform being sent round separately to the artist's studio. A second portrait of the Duke of York in the Royal Collection, where the double chin is more pronounced, a horse whip replaces the telescope, and the figure is placed in an oval, dates from 1766 (Millar 1014). In effect, as might be expected, the first composition was revised or updated for the later portrait.

The surface of the present, earlier painting shows several alterations, particularly to the uniform and also to the outlines of the hat and face. These can be seen with the naked eye, but are even more apparent in the X-rays taken in 1963. The alterations were almost certainly made in order to reflect the Duke's promotion in the Navy during the time the portrait was being painted. He sailed under the command of Lord Howe as a midshipman in 1758 and saw action. The following year he was promoted to the rank of post-Captain on board the *Phoenix*. Subsequently, in 1761 he was made Vice-Admiral of the Blue, serving with Admiral Hawke and, finally, he became an Admiral.

Relations with his elder brother, George III, became increasingly strained after he was passed over for the lucrative sinecure of the see of Osnabrück in favour of the King's second son (see No. 17) and was excluded from the Council of Regency. Associated with the opposition parties, he voted against the government in the House of Lords in 1767. He was described by Lady Louisa Stuart, the sister of Lord Bute, as "silly, frivolous, and heartless, void alike of steadiness and principle; a libertine in his practice, and in society one of those incessant chatterers who must by necessity mutter a vast deal of nonsense". He did, however, undertake the Grand Tour in 1763–64, spending time in Rome, Florence and Venice amongst other places. While on the Grand Tour he was painted by Pompeo Batoni, George Dance and Richard Brompton – all paintings still in the Royal Collection. He died in Monaco while on his way to Rome for a second visit.

## 3
**Sir Joshua Reynolds**
*Alexander Montgomerie,*
*11th Earl of Eglinton*
*(1726–1796)*

Oil on canvas, 76.2 × 63.5 cm (oval)

Millar 1019

*References*: Waterhouse, *Reynolds*, p. 75

*Notes*: 1. Perhaps the drawing last recorded in Lady Thomond's sale, Christie's, 26 May 1821, lot 19.

This may be a fragment of the unfinished full-length portrait for which Reynolds apparently made a preparatory drawing and received payment in 1784.[1] It may have come into George IV's possession already cut down and may conceivably have been further reduced in 1829 before being framed as an oval. It is unlikely to be a sketch for the portrait. The image is almost Hogarthian in its directness and strong characterization and has a touch of humour. The photograph in Richard Redgrave's inventory undertaken for Queen Victoria shows that at some stage during the nineteenth century the image was overpainted, affecting both the background and the dress. A miniature copy in enamel was made by Henry Bone in 1797 and shows further differences (Walker 778).

The sitter is in Highland dress. He was Equerry to Queen Charlotte (1761–69) and Deputy Ranger of Hyde Park and St James's Park (1766–68). He raised the 77th Regiment of Foot which he commanded in the American War of Independence. He was then Colonel of the 51st Regiment of Foot (1767–95) and of the 2nd Dragoons (1795–96).

**4**

**Thomas Gainsborough**
*Henry, Duke of Cumberland (1745–1790) with the Duchess of Cumberland (1743–1808) and Lady Elizabeth Luttrell (died 1799)*

Oil on canvas, 163.8 × 124.5 cm (oval)

Millar 797

*Exhibitions*: Tate Gallery, 1980–81, no. 128

*References*: Waterhouse, *Gainsborough*, no. 178; D. Manning, 'Gainsborough's Duke and Duchess of Cumberland with Lady Luttrell', *The Connoisseur*, June 1973, pp. 85–93; Cormack, no. 60

*Notes*: 1. Christie's, 2 June 1792, lot 74. 2. J. Sunderland and E. Camesasca, *The Complete Paintings of Watteau*, London 1971, nos. 109 and 133.

The Duke and Duchess of Cumberland (for whom see Nos. 1 and 22) are shown walking in the grounds of Cumberland Lodge in Windsor Great Park. Lady Elizabeth Luttrell, the Duchess of Cumberland's sister, is in attendance and seems to be engaged in sketching the couple. Lady Luttrell was notorious for her low moral conduct, her gambling and her ridiculing of George III and Queen Charlotte. She died in Germany. The painting is a late work (ca. 1783–85) apparently painted "at the Duke's instance". It remained in the artist's possession and was exhibited at Schomberg House in 1789 after his death, subsequently being offered in Mrs Gainsborough's sale, when it was most probably acquired by George IV.[1]

There are two preparatory drawings for the composition. The first, in the Royal Collection, indicates that Gainsborough essayed the subject in a rectangular format with the figures seen against a flattened background. The second drawing, which is in the British Museum, is vertical in format with a greater sense of recession and a stronger contrast in light and shade. It was but a short step from this vertical composition to the oval that Gainsborough finally selected. The trees serve to enclose the figures, who are carefully integrated with the setting, which includes an urn positioned between the principal figures and Lady Luttrell. The late date of the painting is confirmed by the fashion of the dresses and the hats. Its mood is strongly reminiscent of Watteau in works such as *La Promenade* or *La Cascade* (private collections).[2]

Within Gainsborough's own œuvre comparison may be made with *The Mall* (Frick Collection, New York) of 1783 (fig. 8) and the projected composition of *The Richmond Water-walk*, which is known from a group of outstanding figure studies and was commissioned by George III but never brought to fruition. The resolution of a difficult composition, quite apart from the arcadian spirit and the dexterous technique, places this picture amongst Gainsborough's finest late works.

## 5
**Sir Joshua Reynolds**
*David Garrick
(1717–1779) as Kitely*

Oil on canvas, 76.8 × 64.1cm

Inscribed on the back of the canvas by the artist: *David Garrick /aet 52 /1768/ JR pinx.*

Millar 1021

*Exhibitions*: Paris, 1985, no. 34; London, 1986, no. 69

*References*: Waterhouse, *Reynolds*, p. 59

*Notes*: 1. Exhibited London, 1986, no. 42. 2. Christie's, 5 June 1812, lot 93.

Garrick was the foremost actor of the eighteenth century, but, more than that, he was a man totally dedicated to the theatre in the sense that he was also involved as manager, playwright and producer. In all of these activities he was eminently successful and often innovative. For example, he revolutionised acting by cultivating a more naturalistic delivery in place of the traditional declamatory, laboured style. Edmund Burke, who owned this portrait, said that Garrick "raised the character of his profession to the rank of a liberal art". Having received his education in Lichfield under Dr Samuel Johnson, Garrick launched his acting career in 1741 in London at Goodman's Fields Theatre where later, after being rejected by both Drury Lane and Covent Garden, he performed many of the major Shakespearean roles – notably the tragedies – to great acclaim. From 1747 Garrick began his association with the management of Drury Lane and in 1749 married the dancer Eva-Marie Veigel (known as Violetti). He retired from the theatre finally in 1776 and is buried in Westminster Abbey.

Garrick recognised the importance of being painted to the furtherance of his career. Hogarth, Zoffany, Reynolds and Gainsborough all depicted the actor, with his wife (as in the Royal Collection, Millar 560), at home, on stage, or in allegorical guise. Many of these images were given wider circulation through engravings. The famous painting by Reynolds, *Garrick between Tragedy and Comedy* (private collection),[1] was painted in 1761 and the equally renowned portrait of *Garrick with the bust of Shakespeare* by Gainsborough (destroyed by fire in 1946) was first exhibited in 1766.

For the present picture Reynolds depicted the actor in the role of the jealous merchant Kitely in Garrick's own revival of Ben Jonson's play *Every Man in His Humour* (1598). A contemporary critic described the characters as dressed in an "olde English Manner", meaning in Van Dyck costume. The moment shown is Act II Scene I, which is dominated by Kitely. Garrick revived the play successfully at Drury Lane in 1751. It was one of his greatest roles and he repeated the performance in the year of his retirement. The style, and especially the tones, of the portrait are reminiscent of Velázquez. Sittings for the artist are described in 1767. An engraving by James Finlayson was published in 1769. It is probably Reynolds's earliest portrayal of an actor in a familiar role. Dr Johnson remarked on the actor's death, "I am disappointed by that stroke of death which has eclipsed the gaiety of nations and impoverished the public stock of harmless pleasure". The portrait was acquired by George IV at Burke's sale.[2]

## 6

**Sir Joshua Reynolds**

*Frederick William Ernest, Count of Schaumburg-Lippe (1724–1777)*

Oil on canvas, 242.6 × 204.5 cm (enlarged on the right while being painted)

Millar 1027

*References*: Waterhouse, *Reynolds*, pp. 19 and 55

The portrait was almost certainly painted as a pendant to No. 11 of the Marquess of Granby, and both may have been commissioned by George, 1st Marquess Townshend (died 1807), who had served on the Continent with both generals, Granby and Lippe, during the Seven Years War (1756–63). The portraits were given by Lady Townshend to George IV, who hung them in the Crimson Drawing Room in Carlton House.

Count Lippe wears on his uniform the ribbon of the Black Eagle of Prussia and he holds a stick in his left hand. Behind him are a cannon, a standard and a page restraining a charger. The count commanded the artillery under Prince Ferdinand of Brunswick during the Seven Years War and later in 1761 was in command of British troops sent to the defence of Portugal. His mother was a daughter of George I by the Duchess of Kendal.

There is evidence from the artist's sitter-books and a subsequent payment that the portrait was painted ca. 1767. It is a relatively early example of Reynold's wholly original approach to portraiture with the setting complementing the figure. There is a pronounced emphasis on the diagonal leading from top left to lower right which is counteracted by the vertical of the figure positioned in the foreground. The opposite diagonal extending from lower left to top right moves from the foreground into the smoke-filled sky suggestive of battle. The figure is seen from below so that the viewer, like the page, looks up at this imposing commander. Reynolds here creates an image of valour by means of composition, pose and an accumulation of military accoutrements. The characterization is suggested by his outward decorum on the field of battle where the essence of the man is most fully revealed. Certain aspects of the design, especially the flag draped over the gun on the left, might have been inspired by the portrait of *Admiral Edward Boscawen* (ca. 1758) by Allan Ramsay (Viscount Falmouth, Tregothnan), but Reynolds's solution is more challenging and he thereby makes the figure more heroic.

## 7
## Sir Joshua Reynolds
*George III when Prince of Wales*

Oil on canvas, 127.6 × 101.6 cm

Millar 1011

*References*: Waterhouse, *Reynolds*, pp. 45–46

*Notes*: 1. Millar 1963, no. 581.

A sitting at 10.00 am on 12 January 1759 given by George III when Prince of Wales to Reynolds is normally associated with this portrait. Reynolds was still trying to establish himself and the year 1759 was an extremely busy one in which he painted over one hundred and fifty sitters. It seems, however, that the canvas was not handed over, since it remained in the artist's studio until his death. The painting then passed into the possession of Reynolds's niece, Mary Palmer, Marchioness of Thomond, who gave it to George IV in 1815.

The Prince of Wales is standing by a table on which his coronet has been placed. He wears an ermine-lined cloak and the ribbon of the Order of the Garter. The representation is to a certain extent comparable with the pastel in the Royal Collection by Jean-Etienne Liotard which forms part of a series commissioned by George III's mother, Augusta, Princess of Wales, in 1754.[1] However, this dignified and restrained, but striking, image produced by Reynolds is perhaps closer to works by Allan Ramsay, who, like Reynolds, was a member of Dr Johnson's circle in London and had already by this date won favour with George III. Ramsay had painted his first full-length portrait of George III when Prince of Wales in 1757 for Lord Bute and this had been reciprocated a year later when the artist was commissioned by the Prince of Wales to paint a portrait of Lord Bute. The success of these portraits (both owned by the National Trust for Scotland, Bute House, Edinburgh) no doubt prompted George III on his accession in 1761 to appoint Ramsay as his Principal Painter (a post he shared with John Shackleton until the latter's death in 1767).

33

## 8
## Sir Joshua Reynolds
*The Death of Dido*

Oil on canvas, 147.3 × 239.4 cm

Millar 1029

*References*: Waterhouse, *Reynolds*, p. 72

*Notes*: 1. R. Dorment, *British Painting in the Philadelphia Museum of Art*, 1986, no. 83.    2. Christie's, 19 May 1821, lot 72.

This important history painting dating from towards the end of Reynolds's life was exhibited at the Royal Academy in 1781. It illustrates an episode recounted by Virgil in the fourth book of *The Aeneid*. Aeneas, while on voyage from Troy to Italy, where he was to found Rome, lands at Carthage and falls in love with the city's widowed queen, Dido. However, he is forced to fulfil his destiny by Jove and so abandons Dido. Anna, Dido's sister, is sent to beg Aeneas to stay, but he ignores her pleas and departs by ship. Distraught, Dido instructs Anna to build a funeral pyre on which are placed all the military spoils brought by Aeneas from Troy, as well as the bed on which Dido slept with her lover. Dido mounts the pyre and falls on Aeneas's sword. Anna rushes forward to embrace her sister in her grief, but Juno sends Iris, the goddess of the rainbow ("saffron-winged, sparkling like dew and trailing a thousand colours as she caught the light of the sun"), to cut a lock of Dido's hair and so release her spirit as she expires. This passage in *The Aeneid* is one of highly charged poetry and Reynolds does it justice, although the picture has suffered from the bituminous contraction of paint. A number of copies exists, the most important of which is the painting in the Philadelphia Museum of Art, where, however, the colour and technique differ.[1] An enamel copy by Henry Bone (No. 29) was made for George IV and two engravings of the composition were also published (see No. 30).

*The Death of Dido* is a perfect demonstration of Reynolds's theory of how the Grand Style should be based on "borrowed attitudes". Scholars have perceived general compositional and iconographical connections with *Dido transfixed with the sword of Aeneas* by Guercino (Palazzo Spada, Rome) and *Herminia discovering the wounded Tancred* also by Guercino (Palazzo Doria-Pamphili, Rome). It has been observed that the pose of Dido, a figure described by Henry Fuseli as one of "supreme beauty in the jaws of death", is close to that adopted by Giulio Romano for his *Sleeping Psyche* in the Sala di Psyche, Palazzo del Tè, Mantua, which in turn is based on the antique sculpture known as *Sleeping Cleopatra* (Rome, Vatican Museums). The figure of Anna is clearly related to a Magdalen figure in a *Lamentation* scene, but, according to a contemporary source, Reynolds had in mind one of the mourning women at the foot of the cross in Daniele da Volterra's *Descent from the Cross* in Santa Trinità dei Monti, Rome. However, as was usually the case with Reynolds, these 'borrowings' were never direct and they had been allowed to percolate through the artist's mind over a considerable period. Indeed, in devising this composition Reynolds was referring back to his years in Rome in 1750–51.

The artist Thomas Stothard visited Reynolds in his studio while he was painting *The Death of Dido*. Reynolds apparently built a pyre of wood on which he placed some drapery and a lay-figure. He later also employed a professional model. Fuseli saw the work in progress and so knew "the throes which it cost its author before it emerged into the beauty, assumed the shape, or was divided into the powerful masses of chia'oscuro which strike us now". The painting remained in Reynolds's studio at his death and was bequeathed to his niece, Mary Palmer, Marchioness of Thomond, at whose sale it was acquired for George IV.[2]

## 9

**Thomas Gainsborough**

*The Three Eldest Princesses: Charlotte, Princess Royal (1766—1828), Augusta (1768—1840) and Elizabeth (1770—1840)*

Oil on canvas, 129.5 × 179.7 cm (an addition of ca. 11.5 cm was made at a later date on the left)

Millar 798

*Exhibitions*: Paris, 1981, no. 56; Cardiff, 1990—91, no. 24

*References*: Waterhouse, *Gainsborough*, no. 135

The Princess Royal is in the centre with Princess Augusta standing to the left and Princess Elizabeth seated on the right. Princess Augusta wears a miniature in a jewelled setting at her breast. The painting was finished early in 1784 and sent specially to Buckingham House for a private view by George III and Queen Charlotte before being submitted to the Royal Academy for public exhibition in the spring. Gainsborough requested that when the painting was hung at the Royal Academy an exception could be made so that the picture should not be positioned too high (i.e. above the level of the tops of the doors, which was standard procedure for full-lengths) because the figures were not painted to be seen at a distance. The Hanging Committee refused his request and Gainsborough withdrew all his paintings from the Royal Academy and never exhibited there again (see Introduction p. 13). *The Three Princesses* was included in the exhibitions Gainsborough organized at Schomberg House in July of the same year and again in 1786.

The portrait was undertaken for George IV and was intended along with Nos. 1 and 22 for display in the Saloon at Carlton House. The format was originally full-length, as seen in the print by Gainsborough Dupont (No. 45) published in 1793. According to Sir Edwin Landseer in conversation with Richard Redgrave in 1868, the canvas was cut down at Windsor Castle at the beginning of the reign of Queen Victoria by the Inspector of Household Deliveries so that it could be used as an overdoor. At the same time it seems that a portion was cut from the top and an addition made to the residue on the left.

On seeing the painting at Schomberg House in the summer of 1784 Gainsborough's staunchest supporter, the Rev. Henry Bate (later the newspaper proprietor Sir Henry Bate-Dudley) wrote a brilliant description of *The Three Princesses* in a review of the exhibition in *The Morning Herald*: "The portraits are recommended by the strict likenesses they exhibit and the very tender and delicate style of pencilling in which they are finished; the features have the softness and beauty of nature, at the nearest approach, with a degree of expression and character that gives animation to the whole. The limbs and other parts are rounded delightfully and sweetly to the eye; but from their being calculated for *tender effect*, should not be surveyed at a great distance. The figures are connected with the utmost harmony and skill, and the drapery finished very highly. Neither strong masses of *light* nor *shade* are to be observed in the composition, and of course the transitions are the gentler and more agreeable. The background is formed of drapery, and a landscape enriched with a beautiful sky."

## 10
### Sir Joshua Reynolds
*Charles Fitzroy, 1st Baron Southampton (1737–1797)*

Oil on canvas, 91.4 × 71.8 cm

Millar 1028

*References*: Waterhouse, *Reynolds*, p.48

The sitter was the grandson of the 2nd Duke of Grafton and spent the first part of his career in the Army, being appointed Ensign in the 1st Foot Guards (1752) and then Captain (1756) and Lieutenant-Colonel (1758). During the Seven Years War (1756–63) he served in Europe as Aide-de-Camp to Prince Ferdinand of Brunswick and was present at the Battle of Minden (1759). His attachment to the Royal Household began as Groom of the Bedchamber to George II and George III (1760–62), Vice-Chamberlain to Queen Charlotte (1768–82), and Groom of the Stole to the Prince of Wales (1780–97). He was, therefore, an early adviser of George IV during the years when the Prince of Wales ran up his first mountainous debts and formed a special relationship with Mrs Fitzherbert that led to a secret marriage ceremony on 15 December 1783, and finally ended in 1794. Southampton's loyalties in these matters were clearly torn between the King and his eldest son. It was said of him by a contemporary that he "had only one fault, to be dislik'd by him [the Prince of Wales] and a blind attachment to the king".

The portrait can be associated with a sitting recorded on 16 January 1760. It is alleged that it was acquired by George IV in 1818 from the dealer Paul Colnaghi, although apparently not delivered to Carlton House until 1822. Lord Southampton is depicted in the state coat (or full dress uniform) of the 1st Foot Guards and holds his hat under his arm.

## 11
**Sir Joshua Reynolds**
*John Manners, Marquess of Granby (1721–1770)*

Oil on canvas, 246.4 × 209.5 cm

Millar 1022

*References*: Waterhouse, *Reynolds*, p. 57

Like No. 6 the portrait may have been commissioned by George, 1st Marquess Townshend (died 1807), who had served with both generals on the Continent during the Seven Years War (1756–63). Both portraits were given by Lady Townshend to George IV who hung them in the Crimson Drawing Room in Carlton House. The sitter was the eldest son of the 3rd Duke of Rutland. He first served under William Augustus, Duke of Cumberland, in subduing the Jacobite rising of 1745. In the present portrait he wears the uniform of Colonel of the Royal Regiment of Horse Guards. He leans against his charger on the other side of which is his page. A battle scene fills the background on the left towards which a detachment of Horse Guards is galloping. As with No. 6, the portrait alludes to the Marquess of Granby's part in the Seven Years War: he began as second-in-command and from 1758 was Commander-in-Chief of the British forces in Germany. He distinguished himself particularly at the Battle of Warburg (1760) when he led a succession of charges against the French lines. Prince Ferdinand of Brunswick publicly thanked the Marquess of Granby, "under whose orders all the British cavalry performed prodigies of valour which they could not fail of doing having his Lordship at their head". Several of the soldiers who fought with him subsequently became publicans and named their inns after him so that the Marquess of Granby remains familiar as an image on inn signs.

The Marquess sat for Reynolds in June 1764 and May 1766. There was a separate sitting for the horse in June 1765. The prime version was exhibited at the Society of Artists in 1766 and was painted for the Maréchal de Broglie: it is now in the John and Mable Ringling Museum, Sarasota. The present painting is a replica which, for the most part, is autograph. The design of the portrait equals that of No. 6 in power of imagination.

12

**Thomas Gainsborough**
*Johann Christian Fischer*
*(1733–1800)*

Oil on canvas, 228.6 × 150.5 cm

Millar 800

*Exhibitions*: Tate Gallery, 1980–81, no. 126; London, 1991–92, no. 63

*References*: Waterhouse, *Gainsborough*, no. 252; M. Postle, 'Gainsborough's "lost" picture of Shakespeare', *Apollo*, December 1991, pp. 374–79; Cormack, no. 50

Fig. 13 Photograph of X-ray composite of No. 12

The sitter was an outstanding musician, a virtuoso oboist and a composer. His oboe is depicted on the harpsichord-cum-piano. The violin on the chair in the background refers to his accomplished performances on that instrument as well. Fanny Burney writes of the "sweet-flowing, melting celestial notes of Fischer's hautboy", but Felice de' Giardini criticized his "impudence of tone".

Fischer was born in Germany and came to London in 1768. He joined Queen Charlotte's band, playing regularly at court. Despite his acclaim, he failed to secure the post of Master of the King's Band. The present portrait stands as testimony to Gainsborough's own love of music, but also had personal significance since Fischer was his son-in-law. The artist seems to have first met the musician in Bath during the mid-1770s. The marriage between Fischer and Gainsborough's elder daughter Mary (1748–1826) took place in London on 21 February 1780. The artist did not have great confidence in Fischer as a husband and he wrote to his sister on 23 February, "I can't say I have any reason to doubt the man's honesty or goodness of heart, as I never heard anyone speak anything amiss of him; and as to his oddities and temper, she must learn to like as she likes his person, for nothing can be altered now. I pray God she may be happy with him and have her health." The marriage did not last and ended in tragedy as Mary became insane.

The portrait is masterly in its skilful composition, strong characterization and vivid colours ("in scarlet, laced, like a Colonel of the Guards"). It was exhibited at the Royal Academy in 1780, but was in all likelihood painted either in Bath or London in 1774. X-rays of the picture (fig. 13), taken by the National Gallery in 1991, confirmed that it had been painted over an abandoned portrait identified as *Shakespeare between Tragedy and Comedy* and probably commissioned by David Garrick in 1768. Gainsborough, who was not sympathetic to allegory, seems to have had difficulty with the projected composition and so appears not to have continued with it.

The portrait of *Johann Christian Fischer* was acquired at an early date by the 4th Earl of Abingdon (died 1799), who was an amateur flautist, and subsequently sold. It was given by Ernest, Duke of Cumberland to his brother George IV in 1809.

## 13
## Thomas Gainsborough
### George III

Oil on canvas, 238.8 × 158.7 cm

Millar 774

*References*: Waterhouse, *Gainsborough*, no. 309

This and the companion portrait of Queen Charlotte (No. 16) were exhibited at the Royal Academy in 1781. Sir Henry Bate-Dudley, writing in *The Morning Herald*, stated of this portrait, "The king's is by far the most striking, and at the same time the most correct and graceful portrait ever given of him". Not all were of this opinion, however. Horace Walpole, for instance, thought that the portrait of George III was "very like, but stiff and raw". Although technically not State Portraits, the images have justly been described as "portraits of grand informality" and were indeed extensively copied. To this extent the portraits do appear to have been regarded as sequels to the State Portraits of George III and Queen Charlotte painted by Allan Ramsay in 1761.

The handling of the portrait of George III is by Gainsborough's standards somewhat restrained even in the treatment of the landscape. The height of the figure is accentuated by the fluted column on the left and the form is silhouetted against the background. The effect is more linear than is usual in Gainsborough's portraits and the whole composition is carefully controlled, even subdued. A mezzotint after the portrait was made by Gainsborough Dupont (No. 41).

George III wears the Windsor uniform with the ribbon and star of the Order of the Garter, and the Garter round his knee. The Windsor uniform was apparently designed by the King himself for the use of his family and friends. It was probably inspired by the hunting livery designed for his father, Frederick, Prince of Wales.

## 14
## Sir Joshua Reynolds
*Cymon and Iphigenia*

Oil on canvas, 143.2 × 172.1 cm

Millar 1030

*References*: Waterhouse, *Reynolds*, p. 81

Like *The Death of Dido* (No. 8), *Cymon and Iphigenia* is an important history painting dating from Reynolds's final years. It was exhibited at the Royal Academy in 1789 and was therefore one of his last works. It was engraved on three separate occasions (No. 32) and an enamel copy was made by Henry Bone (No. 31) for George IV. A smaller, unfinished painted copy by William Etty (see No. 64) is in York City Art Gallery.

The subject is taken from Giovanni Boccaccio's *Decameron* (Day 5, 1st Novella). Reynolds may have used the verse translation made by John Dryden published in his *Fables Ancient and Modern* (1700). Cymon was the backward son of a Cyprian noble who was confined by his father to his country estates. He was "Fair, Tall, his Limbs with due Proportion join'd,/ But of a heavy, dull, degenerate mind". While out wandering on the estate one summer morning, Cymon, carrying "His Quarter Staff, which he cou'd ne'er forsake", found Iphigenia asleep sheltering in a grove by a stream. Cymon was instantly struck by Iphigenia's beauty: "The Fool of Nature" stood "with stupid Eyes/And gaping Mouth that testify'd surprise,/Fix'd on her Face, nor cou'd remove his Sight". The sight civilised and transformed Cymon to the extent that he courted Iphigenia and they eventually married. The subject was also painted by Benjamin West in the 1760s, for George III according to one source.

For the figure of Iphigenia Reynolds has exploited the Venetian tradition of the female nude: the *Venus* by Giorgione in Dresden, the *Venus of Urbino* by Titian in the Uffizi, Florence, the *Venus del Pardo* by Titian in the Louvre, Paris, or *The Andrians* by Titian (Prado, Madrid). These examples are in turn dependent on figures occurring on sarcophagi. To these can be added an awareness of paintings by Correggio such as *Jupiter and Antiope* (Paris, Louvre) and *Jupiter and Io* (Kunsthistorisches Museum, Vienna). The pose of Cymon, who appears at the right of the composition, is reminiscent of the shepherds in Guercino's *Et in Arcadia Ego* (Rome, Galleria Nazionale d'Arte Antica). As with *The Death of Dido*, these correspondences are far from exact and in their different ways relate to separate moments in Reynolds's career. In general terms, however, the composition with its sense of voyeurism again refers back to subjects painted by Titian – *Venus with an organist, Venus with a lute-player, Venus with a mirror, Danaë*.

The painting remained in the artist's studio until his death when it was bequeathed to his niece, Mary Palmer, Marchioness of Thomond, by whom it was presented to George IV in 1814. The condition of the picture seems to have given cause for concern at an early date. William Seguier, who succeeded Benjamin West as Surveyor, refused to clean the painting when it arrived on the grounds "that in attempting to remove [the dirt] we should destroy some of the beautiful glazings". Nonetheless, like *The Death of Dido*, *Cymon and Iphigenia* is a supreme example of Reynolds's powers of composition.

## 15

**Thomas Gainsborough**
*Diana and Actaeon*

Oil on canvas, 158.1 × 188 cm

Millar 806

*Exhibitions*: Tate Gallery, 1980–81,
no. 137

*References*: Waterhouse, *Gainsborough*,
no. 1012; R. Paulson, *Emblem and
Expression: Meaning in English Art of
the Eighteenth Century*, London 1975,
p. 224; J. Hayes, *Gainsborough's
Landscape Paintings*, London 1982, I,
p. 174 and II, no. 160; A. Bermingham,
*Landscape and Ideology: The English
Rustic Tradition 1740–1860*, London
1987, pp. 46, 207; M. Rosenthal,
'Gainsborough's *Diana and Actaeon*', in
*Painting and the Politics of Culture. New
Essays on British Art 1700–1850*, ed.
J. Barrell, Oxford and New York 1992,
pp. 167–194; Cormack, no. 62

*Notes*: 1. J. Hayes, *The Drawings of
Thomas Gainsborough*, London 1970,
nos. 810, 811, 812. 2. Christie's,
10 April 1797, lot 43.

Fig. 14 Study for *Diana and Actaeon*,
black and white chalks and grey and
grey-black washes on buff paper,
256 × 333 mm, private collection

Although not unique in Gainsborough's œuvre (another example is *Musidoro* in the Tate Gallery), the subject-matter of this picture is most unusual for the artist. What is more, the painting is his only surviving mythological subject treated as narrative. It is a very late work (ca. 1785), comparable in some respects with *Lurchers coursing a fox* (The Iveagh Bequest, Kenwood House). *Diana and Actaeon* is often described as unfinished, but this is a moot point and it may well be that Gainsborough had developed the painting as far as he had intended. On occasions the painting has been referred to as a 'sketch', but its size would seem to militate against the use of this term. Although it is somewhat monochromatic, a considerable amount of colour has in fact been applied in small but telling quantities.

There are three preparatory drawings that reveal the evolution of the composition and the care with which Gainsborough approached the task. The first is in a private collection (fig. 14), the second in the Huntington Library and Art Gallery, San Marino, California, and the third in the Cecil Higgins Art Gallery, Bedford.[1] The seated bather below Actaeon on the left of the composition is derived from a bronze of a seated girl by Adriaen de Vries based on the antique, a lead cast of which is in the Victoria and Albert Museum. The same source was also used for the *Musidoro*.

The literary source for *Diana and Actaeon* is the third book of Ovid's *Metamorphoses*, where in a highly charged style the poet recounts the story of Actaeon, who, while out hunting in the sacred valley of Gargaphe, comes across the cave where Diana and her nymphs are bathing in a spring. At the sight of Actaeon Diana throws water in his face whereupon he is transformed into a stag and is eventually torn apart by his own hounds. Gainsborough shows Actaeon with sprouting horns half concealed behind a rock on the left. The subject was a popular one in Renaissance and seventeenth-century European painting: examples by Titian,

Lambert Sustris, Frans Floris, Filippo Lauri and Carlo Maratta were known in England either in the original or through engravings. Similarly, renderings of related subjects on the theme of Diana were undertaken by French artists such as Louis de Boullogne the Younger and Watteau, and these were also known through engravings. It is, however, not a subject that is often found in British art, although Zoffany and Hayman did attempt it during the 1760s. Francis Wheatley's *The Salmon Leap at Leixlip* (1783), now in the Yale Center for British Art, may be relevant since that is also a composition with numerous female bathers.

A recent interpretation of *Diana and Actaeon* concludes that Gainsborough painted the subject as "a critique of Reynolds's academic theories". Such conclusions can usefully be tested in this exhibition by comparing *Diana and Actaeon* with Nos. 8 and 14. It remains a fact that this painting has a resonance beyond the confines of British art, reaching back to Titian and forward to Renoir, Cézanne and Matisse.

*Diana and Actaeon* remained in the artist's studio at his death and was in Gainsborough Dupont's sale when it was acquired by George IV.[2]

## 16

**Thomas Gainsborough**
*Queen Charlotte*

Oil on canvas, 238.8 × 158.7 cm

Millar 775

*References*: Waterhouse, *Gainsborough*, no. 130

The painting forms a pair with No. 13 and is one of the artist's finest portraits. Sir Henry Bate-Dudley, writing in *The Morning Herald*, recorded of this portrait: "The Queen's is the only happy likeness we ever saw portrayed of her Majesty: the head is not only very highly finished but expresses all that amiableness of character which so justly distinguishes her. There is a stiffness in full dress that always cruelly militates against the artist in spite of his best endeavours: this is evident in the above picture, though the drapery is charmingly pencilled and relieved." The greatest praise, however, came from Reynolds's pupil, James Northcote, who recognised that, given Queen Charlotte's plain features, Gainsborough had in fact created a compelling image of female virtues. Northcote also explains that Gainsborough had to finish the portrait at great speed: "'Tis actual motion, and done with such a light, airy facility. It delighted me when I saw it. The drapery was done in one night by Gainsborough and his nephew; they sat up all night, and painted it by candle-light. This in my opinion, constitutes the essence of genius, the making beautiful things from unlikely subjects . . . ."

The success of the portrait of George III (No. 13) and the present work confirmed Gainsborough's position as unofficial court painter and assured him of further royal commissions. A mezzotint of the portrait was made by Gainsborough Dupont (No. 42).

## 17

**Sir Joshua Reynolds**

*Frederick, Duke of York (1763–1827)*

Oil on canvas, 240 × 146.7 cm

Millar 1018

*References*: Waterhouse, *Reynolds*, p. 79

The sitter wears the mantle of the Order of the Garter with the plumed hat of the Order on the table behind. The portrait was in all probability painted for the sitter's elder brother, George IV, and was hung in the Ante-Chamber to the Throne Room of Carlton House, where it was later paired with a not dissimilar portrait of *The Prince of Wales in Garter Robes* by John Hoppner painted in 1796 (Millar 834). Sittings for the artist are recorded in late 1787 and early 1788 when the painting was exhibited at the Royal Academy. An engraving by John Jones was published in 1790. It has been suggested that only the head was painted by Reynolds himself and that an exceptionally good assistant executed the robes and the background. Nonetheless, the work must rank as one of the more successful of Reynolds's royal portraits. The architecture is reminiscent of certain compositions by Paolo Veronese such as *The Family of Darius before Alexander* (National Gallery, London).

Frederick, Duke of York, pursued a career in the Army. After a rigorous training in Germany and a short period of command in the Low Countries in 1793–95, he was appointed Field-Marshal. Three years later he was made Commander-in-Chief of the Army (1798–1809 and 1811–27) where he carried out important reforms and won the respect of the Duke of Wellington. The Duke of York remained George III's favourite son even though he took his elder brother's side in the Regency crisis in 1788–89. He was in many respects as extravagant as George IV, having access to greater personal funds partly accruing from the revenues (£20,000 per annum) of the bishopric of Osnabrück that had accumulated during his minority. He gave up the part-Protestant, part-Catholic bishopric in 1803 and spoke against Catholic emancipation in 1825. In 1791 he married Frederica, eldest daughter of Frederick William II, King of Prussia. He was the subject of several vicious caricatures by James Gillray portraying him as a libertine.

**18**

**Sir Joshua Reynolds**
*Maria, Duchess of*
*Gloucester (1739–1807)*

Oil on canvas, 187.3 × 136.5 cm

Millar 1015

*Exhibitions*: Cardiff, 1990–91, no. 39

*References*: Waterhouse, *Reynolds*, p. 64

*Notes*: 1. Exhibited London, 1986, no.
122.

The painting was exhibited in 1774 at the Royal Academy, where it was placed next to No. 24, a portrait of the sitter's daughter, Princess Sophia Matilda of Gloucester. Both paintings were apparently painted for the Duke of Gloucester and the present portrait was bequeathed by Princess Sophia Matilda to the Prince Consort. A sitting is recorded as early as 1771, but payment was not made until 1779. A number of copies, several in miniature, are known. The pose is reminiscent of the engraving *Melancholia I* by Albrecht Dürer, to whom Reynolds refers in his Sixth Discourse (10 December 1774): "The works of Albert Durer ... afford a rich mass of genuine materials, which wrought up and polished to elegance, will add copiousness to what, perhaps, without such aid, could have aspired only to justness and propriety."

Maria, Duchess of Gloucester, was the illegitimate daughter of Sir Edward Walpole, the elder brother of Horace Walpole. She had three daughters (depicted by Reynolds in *The Ladies Waldegrave* of 1780–81 now in the National Gallery of Scotland[1]) by her first marriage to James, 2nd Earl Waldegrave, and was seven years older than the Duke of Gloucester whom she married secretly in 1766. Only when she became pregnant in 1772 did the Duke of Gloucester inform the King of his marriage. The Duke and Duchess of Gloucester were duly banished from court. The King, being equally goaded by the behaviour of the Duke and Duchess of Cumberland (Nos. 1, 4, 22), introduced the Royal Marriage Act of 1772 making it illegal for members of the Royal Family to marry without the previous consent of the monarch. Financial concerns also put a strain on the previously warm relations between George III and his brother, although eventually the King was reconciled with both the Duke and the Duchess of Gloucester and made provision for their children. George III described the Duchess of Gloucester as a woman of "extreme pride and vanity". She was indeed ambitious and avaricious, but also one of the most beautiful women of her time. She was painted by Reynolds on three other occasions (1761, 1762 and 1764–65) and by Gainsborough (1764–65).

## 19
**Thomas Gainsborough**
*Richard Hurd (1720—1808),
Bishop of Worcester*

Oil on canvas, 75.2 × 62.5 cm (oval)

Millar 801

*Exhibitions*: Cardiff, 1990—91, no. 21

*References*: Waterhouse, *Gainsborough*,
no. 390

The portrait was exhibited at the Royal Academy in 1781 together with Nos. 13 and 16. It was apparently painted for Queen Charlotte. Fanny Burney recorded that Richard Hurd "is, and justly, most high in [the Queen's] favour. In town she has his picture in her bedroom, and its companion is Mrs Delany [by John Opie (Millar 975)]. How worthily paired! what honour to herself, such honour to them! There is no other portrait there but of royal houses." Several versions of the portrait are known, but it should not be confused with another quite similar portrait of the same sitter by Gainsborough also in the Royal Collection (Millar 802).

Richard Hurd was a scholar and critic, who published numerous pamphlets and sermons, a famous critical edition of Horace, and an influential work entitled *Letters on Chivalry and Romance* (1762), which was a forerunner of Romanticism. From 1776 Hurd was put in charge of the education of the Prince of Wales and Duke of York. He had been made Bishop of Lichfield and Coventry in 1774, and became Bishop of Worcester and Clerk of the Closet in 1781, but declined the King's offer of the Archbishopric of Canterbury. Horace Walpole declared that Hurd was "a gentle, plausible man, affecting a singular decorum that endeared him highly to devout old ladies".

## 20
**Sir Joshua Reynolds**
*The Marriage of
George III*

Oil on canvas, 95.2 × 129.5 cm

Millar 1012

*References*: Waterhouse, *Reynolds*,
p. 101

*Notes*: 1. Greenwood's, 16 April 1796,
lot 11.

The marriage between George III and Princess Charlotte of Mecklenburg-Strelitz took place in the Chapel Royal at St James's Palace on the evening of 8 September 1761. The ceremony was performed by the Archbishop of Canterbury. The bride was escorted to the Chapel Royal by two of George III's brothers, the Duke of York (see No. 2) and Prince William (later Duke of Gloucester) and given away by the King's uncle, William Augustus, Duke of Cumberland. There were ten bridesmaids, including Lady Elizabeth Keppel (No. 34). Reynolds positioned himself in a gallery of the Chapel Royal. On the left is a canopy under which the bride and bridegroom sat after the ceremony. Nearby are the Maids of Honour and the Ladies of the Bedchamber. Behind the bride are the bridesmaids. On the right towards the back of the Chapel is George III's mother, Augusta, Princess of Wales, in front of whom are his brothers and sisters; his uncle, William Augustus, Duke of Cumberland, is in the right foreground. The bride wore an "endless mantle of violet-coloured velvet, lined with ermine" and a small tiara of diamonds. The bridegroom is apparently dressed in a silver costume with the collar of the Order of the Garter.

No finished composition seems to have been undertaken. It is conceivable that the artist was hoping to win royal support with such a painting, particularly after his earlier portrait of George III (No. 7), but the oil-sketch remained in Reynolds's studio at his death after which it was sold.[1]

21

**Thomas Gainsborough**

*Charles, 2nd Earl and 1st Marquess Cornwallis (1738–1805)*

Oil on canvas, 76.2 × 63.5 cm (oval)

Millar 799

*Exhibitions*: Cardiff, 1990–91, no. 22

*References*: Waterhouse, *Gainsborough*, no. 167

A similar portrait of the same sitter dating from 1783 and painted for the Marquess of Hastings (see No. 37) is in the National Portrait Gallery. It is likely that the present portrait, which was commissioned from the artist by George IV, dates from the same decade.

Cornwallis is depicted wearing the uniform of a Lieutenant-General. Gazetted Ensign in the Grenadier Guards in 1756, he served in the Seven Years War (1756–63) when he was Aide-de-Camp to the Marquess of Granby (No. 11) and commanded the 12th Regiment of Foot taking part in the Battle of Minden (1759). He was then Aide-de-Camp to George III (1765–66). He served from 1776 in the American War of Independence, in which he had seven regiments under his command, but was forced to capitulate at Yorktown in 1781 bringing the war to a close. Thereafter, he was appointed Governor-General and Commander-in-Chief in India (1786–93), where he reformed both the army and the civil service and won the third Mysore war against Tippoo Sultan. He was Lord-Lieutenant and Commander-in-Chief in Ireland (1798–1801). Cornwallis had a distinguished career, but history has remained ambivalent about his achievements.

## 22
**Thomas Gainsborough**
*Anne, Duchess of Cumberland (1743–1808)*

Oil on canvas, 127.6 × 101.9 cm

Millar 796

*References*: Waterhouse, *Gainsborough*, no. 181

*Notes*: 1. Christie's 10 April 1797, lot 24.

The portrait was intended to form a pair with No. 1, of the Duke of Cumberland. Both were being painted in 1783, but have been brought to different degrees of finish. If No. 1 can be considered the first stage of Gainsborough's working procedure when painting a portrait, then the present image reveals subsequent developments. The face is almost completely finished, whilst the dress is depicted with bravura brushstrokes that reveal the dazzling speed and rhythm that Gainsborough used for such passages during his later years. It is clear that the artist concentrated first on the head and the area around it, before developing the form of the figure itself or the setting.

Both No. 1 and this portrait were painted for George IV and, together with No. 9, were intended for display in the Saloon at Carlton House. However, the portraits of the Duke and Duchess of Cumberland were left unfinished at Gainsborough's death, although all three portraits were on public view at Schomberg House in July 1784. The present portrait, like No. 1, was included in Gainsborough Dupont's sale where it was acquired by George IV.[1]

## 23
**Thomas Gainsborough**
*The Royal Family*

Top row, left to right:

*George III*

*Queen Charlotte*

*George IV when Prince of Wales
(1762–1830)*

*Prince William, later Duke of
Clarence and William IV
(1765–1837)*

*Charlotte, Princess Royal
(1766–1828)*

Middle row:

*Prince Edward, later Duke of Kent
(1767–1820)*

*Princess Augusta (1768–1840)*

*Princess Elizabeth (1770–1840)*

*Prince Ernest, later Duke of
Cumberland (1771–1852)*

*Prince Augustus, later Duke of
Sussex (1773–1843)*

Bottom row:

*Prince Adolphus, later Duke of
Cambridge (1774–1850)*

*Princess Mary (1776–1857)*

*Princess Sophia (1777–1848)*

*Prince Octavius (1779–83)*

*Prince Alfred (1780–82)*

Oil on canvas, each ca. 59 × 44 cm
(oval)

Millar 778–792

*References*: Waterhouse, *Gainsborough*,
nos. 310, 132, 703, 726, 134, 406, 22,
238, 175, 643, 109, 471, 625, 527, 12
respectively

*Prince Edward,*
*later Duke of Kent*

*Princess Elizabeth*

*Prince Octavius*

The portraits were in all probability commissioned by Queen Charlotte and they were first hung in her apartments in Buckingham House. The sittings took place in September and October 1782 at Windsor Castle. A portrait of the King's second son, Frederick, Duke of York (No. 17), was omitted because he was in Hanover. Prince William was at sea, but Gainsborough based the likeness on a slightly earlier portrait now in a private collection in New York. Prince Alfred had died on 20 August 1782 before Gainsborough travelled to Windsor Castle and so the portrait was "painted by remembrance". Prince Octavius died on 3 May 1783 so that the visit by Queen Charlotte and her daughters to see the portraits when they were exhibited in the Royal Academy in 1783 was particularly harrowing and apparently reduced them to tears. The King, the Prince of Wales, Prince Edward, Prince Ernest, Prince Augustus and Prince Adolphus are all depicted wearing Windsor uniform (see No. 13). The King and the Prince of Wales also wear the insignia of the Order of the Garter. Prince William wears naval uniform with the star of the Order of the Thistle. The image of the King was often copied (see No. 39).

The hanging of *The Royal Family* at the Royal Academy exercised Gainsborough considerably. He gave a strong hint to the Hanging Committee that the portraits should not be hung "above the line along with full-lengths" and that if that happened "he never more, whilst he breathes, will send another Picture to the Exhibition". The artist also made a drawing of how the portraits should be assembled "with the Frames touching each other, in this order" (fig. 15). In iconographical terms *The Royal Family* forms a link between the portraits of the children of Charles I by Van Dyck and those of the children of Queen Victoria by Franz Xaver Winterhalter. Henry Angelo states that his father Domenico, the fencing-master, recalled that Gainsborough "was all but raving mad with ecstasy in beholding such a constellation of youthful beauty" and this is reflected in the abandon with which the paint is applied in passages of these portraits.[1]

*Notes*: 1. Henry Angelo, *Reminiscences*, London 1828, I, pp. 191–93.

Fig. 15 Letter from the artist to the Hanging Committee of the Royal Academy illustrating the arrangement of the ovals comprising No. 23, Royal Academy of Arts, London

## 24

**Sir Joshua Reynolds**

*Princess Sophia Matilda of Gloucester (1773–1844)*

Oil on canvas, 63.5 × 77.5 cm

Millar 1016

*References*: Waterhouse, *Reynolds*, p. 64

*Notes*: 1. *The Works of John Ruskin*, ed. E.T. Cook and A. Wedderburn, XXII, *The Eagle's Nest*, London 1906, pp. 225–28.

Princess Sophia Matilda was the daughter of the Duke and Duchess of Gloucester and was therefore a niece of George III. The painting was exhibited in 1774 at the Royal Academy, where it was hung alongside Reynolds's portrait of her mother (No. 18). An engraving by Thomas Watson was published in the following year and there are some partial copies in miniature (Walker 212, 305). Payments were not made to Reynolds until 1779. The portrait was bequeathed by the sitter's sister-in-law, Mary, Duchess of Gloucester, to Queen Victoria in 1857.

Reynolds was particularly successful in capturing the innocence of children and the juxtaposition of the young princess's face with that of the Maltese dog is both charming and humorous. As an image it is comparable, for example, with the portrait of *Miss Jane Bowles* in the Wallace Collection, London, dating from ca. 1775.

John Ruskin discussed this picture in a lecture entitled *The Relation to Art of the Sciences of Organic Form*, given in Oxford in 1872. He said of Reynolds on that occasion, "The absolute truth of outer aspect, and of inner mind, he seizes infallibly; but there is one part of the creatures which he never, for an instant, thinks of, or cares for, — their bones", referring to Reynold's inability to draw accurately.[1]

## 25
### *After* **Sir Joshua Reynolds**
*Samuel Johnson (1709–1784)*

Mezzotint by William Doughty (1757–1782),
45.5 × 33 cm; 2nd state

Published by W. Doughty on 24 June 1779

*References*: Hamilton, p. 42

The portrait on which this print is based was in all probability one of those painted for Johnson's friend Henry Thrale. The portraits were intended for display in the library at Streatham House and were undertaken in 1779. The others were of Oliver Goldsmith (see No. 26) and Dr. Charles Burney (National Portrait Gallery). The portrait of Samuel Johnson is in the Tate Gallery. Unlike No. 28, the pose adopted on this occasion shows Johnson dressed in ordinary clothes and in conversation. This presumably is how he would have been seen by Reynolds and his friends at the Literary Club (see Introduction, p. 6), and the viewer is immediately conscious of the writer's powers of concentration and interlocution.

## 26
### *After* **Sir Joshua Reynolds**
*Oliver Goldsmith (1730–1774)*

Mezzotint by Giuseppe Marchi (1735–1808),
45.5 × 33 cm; 2nd state

Published by R. Sayer 1 December 1770

*References*: Hamilton, p. 32

*Notes*: 1. Exhibited London, 1986, no. 79.

Goldsmith, author of the novel *The Vicar of Wakefield* (1766), the poem *The Deserted Village* (1770), and plays such as *She Stoops to Conquer* (1773), was a founder member of the Literary Club and one of Reynolds's closest friends. James Northcote described the writer's death as "the severest blow Sir Joshua ever received – he did not paint all that day".

Reynolds seems to have painted Goldsmith in 1768–69 and the portrait (now at Knole) was exhibited at the Royal Academy in 1770 to form a pair with a portrait of Johnson (see No. 28). An autograph version was executed for Henry Thrale at Streatham Park.[1] The pose and mode of dress (reminiscent of seventeenth-century fashion) were deemed by Reynolds to be appropriate for writers and artists.

## 27
### *After* Sir Joshua Reynolds
*The Rev. Laurence Sterne (1713–1768)*

Mezzotint by Edward Fisher (1722–ca. 1785),
38 × 27.5 cm; 1st state

Published by E. Fisher in 1761

*References*: Hamilton, p. 66

*Notes*: 1. Painting exhibited London, 1986, no. 37.

Reynolds undertook the portrait of Sterne in 1760 during the publication of the first volumes of the novel-ist's most famous work, *The Life and Opinions of Tristram Shandy* (seen in the print among the manu-scripts on the table). The novel caused a sensation and it is interesting that as soon as the portrait was finished Reynolds had it engraved by Fisher for immediate sale, probably as a speculative venture. The portrait (now in the National Portrait Gallery) was twice shown at the Society of Artists: 1761 (together with the print) and 1768.[1] The sitter is depicted in clerical garb and in a contemplative pose (somewhat undermined by the faintly cynical smile) which Reynolds favoured for his early portraits of writers.

## 28
### *After* Sir Joshua Reynolds
*Samuel Johnson*

Mezzotint by James Watson (ca. 1739–1790),
45.5 × 33 cm; 1st state

Published by R. Sayer

*References*: Hamilton, p. 41

*Notes*: 1. Exhibited London, 1986, no. 73.

This print was taken from a portrait painted in 1769 and acquired by the Duke of Dorset in the same year; it is still at Knole.[1] The date, size and composition make it clear that it was painted as a pair with the portrait of Oliver Goldsmith (No. 26). Both were shown at the Royal Academy in 1770 and honour the appointments of Johnson and Goldsmith as Professor of Ancient Literature and Professor of Ancient History respec-tively. The composition is unusual for Reynolds, who has positioned himself close to the sitter and observed him in profile (in contrast to No. 25). The result is an intimate image of Johnson, who is shown as a seer or sage — "a mind preying on itself". Johnson met Rey-nolds ca. 1754 and Boswell in 1763, and it is from these friendships that so much of Johnson as a scholar and personality is revealed either in paint or in prose.

## 29
### *After* Sir Joshua Reynolds
Henry Bone (1755–1834)
*The Death of Dido*

Signed and dated lower right: *H.Bone 1804*

Enamel, 25.0 × 33.3 cm

Walker 790

The enamel is a copy of No. 8 of which a print (No. 30) was also made. An inscription by Bone on the back reads: "London April 1804 / retouched June 1804 / Painted for His Royal Highness the Prince of Wales / by Henry Bone A.R.A. Enamel Painter to H.R.H. / after the Picture by the late Sir Joshua Reynolds / painted in the Year 1786 [*sic*], in the possession of the / Most Noble the Marchioness of Thomond / Size of the Picture 7 feet 10 inches by 4 feet 10 / N.B. On the left hand of the Iris are five / fingers and a thumb." The preparatory drawing by Bone is in the library of the National Portrait Gallery.

The enamel was hung in George IV's Private Bedroom in Carlton House several years before he acquired the painting. Contrary to the date given in the inscription, the year that *The Death of Dido* was exhibited at the Royal Academy was 1781.

## 30
### *After* Sir Joshua Reynolds
*The Death of Dido*

Mezzotint by Joseph Grozer (ca. 1755–before 1799), 49.5 × 59.5 cm; 1st state (?)

Published by J. Grozer on 9 May 1796

*References*: Hamilton, p. 146

The print is after No. 8, of which an enamel was also made by Henry Bone (No. 29). Notations made by Reynolds in his pocket-books indicate that the artist approached William Doughty in 1779 and William Dickinson in 1781 to engrave the composition, but in the event a print was not published until 1796, four years after Reynolds's death.

### 31
### *After* Sir Joshua Reynolds
Henry Bone
*Cymon and Iphigenia*

Signed and dated lower right: *H.Bone/1806*

Enamel, 24.5 × 33.1 cm

Walker 792

The enamel is a copy of No. 14, which was exhibited at the Royal Academy in 1789. An inscription by Bone on the back reads: "Cymon and Iphigenia / London March 1806 / Painted for His Royal Highness the Prince of Wales by / Henry Bone A.R.A. Enamel painter to His R.H. / after the Original by the late Sir Joshua Reynolds / in the possession of the Most Noble the Marchioness of Thomond." Bone's preparatory drawing is in the library of the National Portrait Gallery. The print (No. 32) after the composition dates from several years after the enamel.

Like *The Death of Dido* (No. 29), *Cymon and Iphigenia* was hung in George IV's Private Bedroom in Carlton House.

### 32
### *After* Sir Joshua Reynolds
*Cymon and Iphigenia*

Engraving with etching by William Overend Geller (exhibited between 1834 and 1846) and Francis Haward (1759–1797), 47.2 × 52 cm

Printed by S.H. Hawkins; published by W.O. Geller on 1 September 1835

The composition by Reynolds (No. 14) was engraved on two previous occasions by Francis Haward (1797) and S.W. Reynolds, but only after Reynolds's death. The painting was exhibited four times in the early nineteenth century at the British Institution (1813, 1826, 1827 and 1833). Geller's print would seem to reflect the popularity of *Cymon and Iphigenia* at that time.

**33**

**After Sir Joshua Reynolds**
*"Count Hugolino and his Children in the Dungeon, as described by Dante in the thirty-third Canto of the Inferno"*

Mezzotint by John Dixon (before 1740–1811), 50.5 × 62 cm; 2nd state

Published by J. Boydell on 4 February 1774

*References*: Hamilton, p. 159

*Notes*: 1. Exhibited London, 1986, no. 82.  2. Cf. N. Penny, *Catalogue of European Sculpture in the Ashmolean Museum, 1540 to the Present Day*, 3 vols, I, Oxford 1992, no. 72, p. 95f.

The title is as given by Reynolds when the painting was exhibited at the Royal Academy in 1773. It was acquired in 1775 by the Duke of Dorset, who was a frequent buyer of Reynolds's history and fancy paintings, and is still at Knole.[1] The figure of Ugolino is undoubtedly inspired by Michelangelo (for example, the *Ancestors of Christ* in the Sistine Chapel), but other aspects of the compositon, such as the treatment of the light, are reminiscent of Caravaggio (for example, *The Calling of St Matthew* in San Luigi dei Francesi, Rome).

The subject may have been suggested to Reynolds by a passage written by Jonathan Richardson the Elder in his *Two Discourses* (1719), describing a sixteenth-century Italian relief sculpture illustrating the passage in Dante (*Inferno*, Canto XXXIII, 1–90) in which Count Ugolino recounts his despair on realising that his imprisonment would ultimately involve him in making the choice between starving to death or surviving by eating his own children after they had died. In the end "fasting had more power than grief". The relief sculpture seen by Richardson was then thought to have been by Michelangelo, but it is in fact by Pierino da Vinci and exists in bronze, wax, and terracotta.[2]

**34**

*After* **Sir Joshua Reynolds**
*Lady Elizabeth Keppel (1739–1768)*

Mezzotint by Edward Fisher, 59 × 36.5 cm; 2nd state

Published by E. Fisher in 1761

*References*: Hamilton, p. 113

The sitter was the daughter of the Earl and Countess of Albemarle and in 1764 married Francis, Marquess of Tavistock. She was the sister of Reynolds's friend and patron Commodore Augustus Keppel (No. 35). The print is based on a painting exhibited at the Society of Artists in 1762 and now at Woburn Abbey. The dress is that worn by Lady Keppel at the wedding of George III and Queen Charlotte (see No. 20) and the action of adorning the bust of Hymen (the Roman god of marriage), who holds a crown, is a further allusion to that event.

This magnificent mezzotint was published at an unusually high price (15 shillings), comparable with the print of *Ugolino* (No. 33).

**35**

*After* **Sir Joshua Reynolds**
*The Hon. Augustus Keppel (1725–1786)*

Mezzotint by Edward Fisher, 50.5 × 35.4 cm; 2nd state

Inscribed in the lower margin: *The Honourable Augustus Keppel commanding His Majesty's Ship Torbay, Nov 20 1759*

*References*: Hamilton, p. 43

*Notes*: 1. Exhibited London, 1986, no. 19.

Augustus Keppel was the son of the 2nd Earl of Albemarle and had a distinguished though controversial (see No. 47) career in the Navy, ultimately becoming First Lord of the Admiralty (1782). Having invited Reynolds to sail with him to the Mediterranean in 1749, he became an influential figure in Reynolds's life. The portrait from which this print was made, painted not long after Reynolds returned from Italy in 1752, established the artist's reputation. It is now in the National Maritime Museum.[1] The figure is inspired by the antique statue of the Apollo Belvedere, although Reynolds has adapted the pose.

## 36
### *After* Sir Joshua Reynolds
### *"View from Sir Joshua Reynolds's House, Richmond Hill"*

Mezzotint by John Jones (active 1775–1797), 49.7 × 56.7 cm

Published by E. Jones and Messrs. Colnaghi and Co. on 1 February 1800

*References*: Hamilton, p. 155

*Notes*: 1. Exhibited London, 1986, no. 99.

The title used is that given when the subject was first engraved by William Birch in 1788 (1 July). Jones entitled his slightly later print *A View of Petersham & Twickenham Meadows from Richmond Hill.* Reynolds built Wick House on Richmond Hill to designs by Sir William Chambers (see No. 56) in 1771–72. The artist, however, had little interest in landscape, in striking contrast with Gainsborough, who, as it happens, died in the year in which the painting on which this print is based was executed. The painting is in the Tate Gallery.[1] Earlier critics made the comparison with landscapes by Rembrandt, but more recently it has been seen as an exercise in the Picturesque perhaps influenced by Claude Lorrain — albeit a limited exercise, since the painting is the only surviving landscape that can be certainly attributed to Reynolds and in general he did not involve himself with such subject-matter except where necessary in the backgrounds to portraits. The poet Samuel Rogers, who owned the painting, stated that when he spent time at Richmond Reynolds "always wanted to get back to town among *people*".

**37**

***After* Sir Joshua Reynolds**
*Francis Rawdon-Hastings, 2nd Earl of
Moira and 1st Marquess of Hastings
(1754–1826)*

Mezzotint by John Jones, 65.9 × 43.5 cm; 1st state

Published by John Jones on 1 May 1792

*References*: Hamilton, p. 56

The portrait was one of the last painted by Reynolds
from sittings; these are recorded in 1789. Progress on
the portrait was widely observed because of the
increasing difficulties that Reynolds had with his eyes.
However, Reynolds has produced one of his finest full-
length portraits in the heroic mould. It was shown at
the Royal Academy to great acclaim in 1790. The
painting was commissioned by Frederick, Duke of York
(see No. 17) and acquired by George IV at the Duke of
York's sale:[1] it is still in the Royal Collection (fig. 12).[2]

**38**

***After* Sir Joshua Reynolds**
*Lieutenant-Colonel Tarleton (1754–1833)*

Mezzotint by John Raphael Smith (1752–1812),
64 × 39.5 cm; 2nd state

Published by J.R. Smith on 11 October 1792

*References*: Hamilton, p. 67

The print is one of the finest made after a painting by
Reynolds. The painter himself remarked, "It has every-
thing but the colour". The portrait was painted in 1782
and exhibited in the Royal Academy in the same year.
It is now in the National Gallery. The pose begs comparison with the antique statue in the Louvre believed
in the eighteenth century to represent Cincinnatus.
Horace Walpole remarked of the man: "Tarleton boasts
of having butchered more men and lain with more
women than anybody else in the army".

*Notes*: 1. Christie's, 7 April 1827, lot 107. 2. Millar 1969,
no. 1023; exhibited London, 1986, no. 153.

**39**

**John Downman (1750–1824)**

*George III*

Signed and dated: *J Downman / Pt. 1787*

Pencil and watercolour with stump heightened with white,
21.6 × 17.5 cm. (oval)

**40**

**John Downman**

*Queen Charlotte*

Signed and dated: *J Downman / Pt. 1787.*

Pencil and watercolour with stump heightened with white,
22.9 × 19.1 cm

Nos. 39 and 40 form a pair and were reputedly given by George III to the royal jeweller François Jean Duval. Downman made several portraits of Queen Charlotte. The King is depicted wearing Windsor uniform with the star and ribbon of the Order of the Garter. The image is based on the full-length portrait by Gainsborough of 1781 (No. 13), which served as a prototype for numerous copies in oil and in miniature.

The drawings were acquired by the Royal Collection at auction in 1992.

## 41
### *After* **Thomas Gainsborough**
*George III*

Mezzotint by Gainsborough Dupont (1754–1797),
62.7 × 37.8 cm; 2nd state

Published by Gainsborough Dupont on 30 December 1790

*References*: Chaloner Smith, II, p.240, Dupont no. 6

This is a print after the portrait of George III by
Gainsborough (No. 13) exhibited at the Royal
Academy in 1781.

Gainsborough Dupont was the nephew of Thomas
Gainsborough and was apprenticed to his uncle in
1772 in Bath, subsequently moving to London. He was
always closely associated with all aspects of his uncle's
work and indeed produced several replicas of the portraits of George III and Queen Charlotte. He exhibited
in his own right at the Royal Academy from 1790 until
his death.

## 42
### *After* **Thomas Gainsborough**
*Queen Charlotte*

Mezzotint by Gainsborough Dupont, 62.3 × 37.7 cm; 1st
state

Published by Gainsborough Dupont on 4 June 1790

*References*: Chaloner Smith, II, p. 238, Dupont no. 2

The print is after the portrait of Queen Charlotte by
Gainsborough (No. 16), exhibited at the Royal
Academy in 1781 and forming a pair with the portrait
of the King (Nos. 13 and 41). An oil-sketch by
Gainsborough Dupont, after the portrait formerly in
the possession of the late Princess Alice, Countess of
Athlone, was probably made in connection with the
preparatory process for the print.

been given to John Hayes St Leger who George IV described as "one of ye best fellows yet ever lived".

George IV wears a uniform of his own invention since he was not commissioned into the Army by his father until 1794–95. He wears the star of the Order of the Garter which is also on the shabracque.

J.R. Smith was considered to be the outstanding mezzotinter of his day and this print was one of his most popular, being re-engraved on four occasions. Consequently there was a large number of proofs.

## 43

### *After* Thomas Gainsborough
*George IV when Prince of Wales*

Mezzotint by John Raphael Smith, 65.5 × 45.5 cm

Published by J.R. Smith on 28 April 1783

*References*: Chaloner Smith, III, p. 1308, J.R. Smith no. 167

The painting on which this mezzotint and the enamel (No. 44) are based is now at Waddesdon Manor (The National Trust, The James A. de Rothschild Collection). It was commissioned by George IV from Gainsborough on behalf of his boon companion John Hayes St Leger and sent to the latter's uncle, General Anthony St Leger (died 1786, the founder of the classic horse race). At the same time George IV commissioned a portrait of John Hayes St Leger (fig. 10) as a pair, although the portraits never seem to have been shown as such after they had both been included in the Royal Academy exhibition of 1782. It is worth bearing in mind that George IV was still only twenty years old when he commissioned these important late portraits from the artist. Gainsborough was instructed to include the shabracque in both paintings. The shabracque had

## 44

### *After* Thomas Gainsborough
Jacob Miltenberg (active 1776–1796)
*George IV when Prince of Wales*

Signed and dated on the back: *J.J. Miltenberg, pinxit / Londini 1784.*

Enamel, 7.5 × 6.2 cm (oval)

Walker 285

Miltenberg was almost certainly of Swiss origin, but he worked mainly in London. The enamel is after the portrait commissioned by George IV from Gainsborough in 1782 for John Hayes St Leger (see No. 43).

## 45

### *After* **Thomas Gainsborough**
### *The Three Eldest Princesses: Charlotte, Princess Royal, Augusta and Elizabeth*

Mezzotint by Gainsborough Dupont, 66. × 45.5 cm; 2nd state

Published by Gainsborough Dupont on 2 September 1793

*References*: Chaloner Smith, II, p. 240, Dupont no. 5

The print records the composition of the painting by Gainsborough (No. 9) commissioned by George IV and finished in 1784 before it was cut down during the reign of Queen Victoria so that it could serve as an overdoor. An oil-sketch by Gainsborough Dupont after the painting is in the Victoria and Albert Museum and may have some connexion with the preparatory stages of the print.

**46**

*After* **Sir Joshua Reynolds**
*George IV when Prince of Wales*

Stipple engraving by Francis Haward,
49.4 × 51.7 cm; 2nd state

Published by F. Haward on 18 January
1793

*References*: Hamilton, p. 70

*Notes*: 1. Waterhouse, *Reynolds*, p. 75.
2. Formerly collection of the Marquess
of Londonderry, sold Sotheby's, 16
November 1988, lot 73.

The original portrait by Reynolds was exhibited at the Royal Academy
exhibition of 1784. The critic in *The Morning Herald* opined that "The
promise Sir Joshua made in his portrait of Col. Tarleton [No. 38] is badly
kept by his performance of the Prince." The painting is now in the collection of Lord Brocket.[1] Contrary to the opinion expressed by the reviewer
in the *The Morning Herald*, the portrait is an important item in the personal
iconography of George IV, since it depicts him memorably as though on
the field of battle, a role that he particularly sought as the Napoleonic wars
spread, but was expressly forbidden by his father. In fact, the role of active
military leader eluded him totally, a disappointment that by the end of his
life made him prey to his fantasies. Reynolds creates a romanticised image
that in some respects anticipates works by Géricault such as the *Wounded
cuirassier* (Louvre, Paris). It was comparatively rare for him to give such
prominence to the horse. The composition, for example, has greater dyna-
mism than the portrait of the Marquess of Granby (No. 11). Besides Reynolds only Sir Thomas Lawrence answered George IV's demands for
heroic imagery, by painting him in Field Marshal's uniform in 1814.[2]

## 47

### *After* Sir Joshua Reynolds
### *Thomas, Lord Erskine*

Mezzotint by John Jones, 50.5 × 35 cm; 3rd state

Published by John Jones on 6 May 1786

*References*: Hamilton, p. 26

The original portrait was painted during the early months of 1786 and shown at the Royal Academy in the same year. It was given by the sitter to George IV and is still in the Royal Collection (Millar 1020).

Called to the bar in 1778, Erskine successfully defended Viscount Keppel (see No. 35) who was court-martialled in 1778 for his conduct at the Battle of Ushant. He was appointed Lord Chancellor in 1806. Having been a member of the Commission of Enquiry that undertook the "Delicate Investigation" into the moral conduct of Caroline of Brunswick when Princess of Wales (1806), he later defended her against the Bill of Pains and Penalties in 1820 when George IV attempted to secure a divorce. Lord Erskine was a brilliant but mercurial character. Reynolds said after painting his portrait, "There is a wildness in his eye, approaching to madness, such as I scarcely ever met with in any other instance".

## 48

### Thomas Gainsborough
### *Portrait of a bearded man in a cap (after Rembrandt)*

Oil on canvas, 76.2 × 63.8 cm

Millar 807

*References*: Waterhouse, *Gainsborough*, no. 1062

About twenty copies after the old masters by Gainsborough have survived. The original portrait of a *Bearded man in a cap* dating in all probability from 1657 is now in the National Gallery, London, but was previously in the collection of the 4th Duke of Argyll. Gainsborough painted the Duke of Argyll in 1767 (now in the Scottish National Gallery, Edinburgh) and it is possible that the copy was painted at about this time. A mezzotint of the original by Rembrandt was made by Thomas Watson.

# Books and Manuscripts

## 49

### Sir Joshua Reynolds

*A Discourse, delivered to the Students of the Royal Academy, on the distribution of the prizes, December 10, 1778. By the President*

London, Thomas Cadell, Printer to the Royal Academy, 1779

This copy of the Eighth Discourse was presented by Sir Joshua Reynolds to the historian Edward Gibbon. Bound in is a copy of the Ninth Discourse delivered on 16 October 1780 and published in 1781, which was also presented to Gibbon by Reynolds.

## 50

### Sir Joshua Reynolds

*The Discourses of Sir Joshua Reynolds; illustrated by Explanatory Notes and Plates by Sir John Burnet, FRS*

London, 1842

(No. 50)

John Burnet (1784–1868) was a painter, engraver and theorist. The illustration is from the Eleventh Discourse in which Reynolds returns to the subject of genius and refers to works by Raphael and Titian. The illustration chosen by Burnet for this discourse is a detail from *The Martyrdom of St Peter Martyr* by Titian, dating from 1526–30. The altarpiece was in the church of Santi Giovanni e Paolo, Venice, but was burnt in 1867.

## 51

### Sir Joshua Reynolds

*The Works of Sir Joshua Reynolds, Knt. Late President of the Royal Academy: containing his Discourses, Idlers, A Journey to Flanders and Holland, (now first published,) and his commentary on Du Fresnoy's Art of Painting; printed from his revised copies (with his last corrections and additions,) in 2 volumes to which is added on Account of the Life and Writings of the Author, By Edmond Malone Esq.*

London, T. Cadell, 1797

This is the first complete edition of Reynolds's literary works. A revised edition was issued in 1798 in three volumes. Both volumes were bound for George III and stamped with the King's arms. The second volume is open at Discourse XIV (pp. 194–95), on Gainsborough. Edmond Malone (1741–1812) was trained as a barrister, but became a man of letters on settling in London in 1777. He joined the Literary Club in 1782 and edited the works of Shakespeare and Dryden as well as of Reynolds, whom he knew well (see No. 54).

## 52

*The Microcosm of London*: Drawing from Life at the Royal Academy, Somerset House

London, R.A. Ackermann, 1808

Rudolph Ackermann (1764–1834) was the foremost publisher of colour-plate books in London during the early nineteenth century. *The Microcosm of London* was his first topographical work and was in three volumes illustrated with 103 plates. The preparatory drawings were done by Augustus Pugin and Thomas Rowlandson. This is the presentation copy for George IV when Prince of Wales and bears the bookplate of the Carlton House library.

(No. 52)

## 53

*A Catalogue of the Remaining Part of a Valuable Collection of Curiosities comprising Carvings in Ivory, Trinkets, Coins, Porcelain and Furniture and paintings by Van Huysman and Gainsborough*

Christie's, Monday 24 May 1819 and two following days

*Notes.* 1. Cf. J. Hayes, *The Drawings of Thomas Gainsborough*, London 1970, pp. 95 and 188, no. 343.

There were three sales of Queen Charlotte's collection held anonymously at Christie's in 1819, on 7, 17 and 24 May. The third sale held on 24 May included several drawings by Gainsborough and the portrait of *Carl Friedrich Abel* now in the Huntington Library and Art Gallery, San Marino. Two more drawings were sold in a further anonymous sale held at Christie's on 13 July 1819. Altogether Queen Charlotte owned twenty-two drawings by Gainsborough. The present whereabouts of the drawings is not known.[1]

## 54

## Joseph Farington (1747–1821)

*Diary*, June 1794–November 1795, folios 107–08

Manuscript

The entry for Wednesday 29 October 1794 records the visit of Gainsborough's nephew, Gainsborough Dupont, who discusses with Farington the course of the artist's final illness, his relationship with Reynolds and his predilection for painting by candlelight.

## Joseph Farington

*Diary*, November 1795–August 1796, Folio 105

Manuscript

The entry for Thursday 21 January 1796 records a conversation with Edmond Malone, the friend and first editor of Reynolds's literary works (see No. 51). Malone discusses with Farington aspects of the artist's character and his state of mind at the time of his death.

Farington was born near Manchester, but moved to London in 1763 where he entered the studio of the landscape painter Richard Wilson. There are relatively few paintings by Farington, who was essentially a topographical artist with a preference for drawings usually made for engraving. He began as a member of the Society of Artists (elected 1765), but twenty years later became a Royal Academician. It is, in fact, with the policies and activities of the Royal Academy that he is most closely associated, mainly through his *Diary*. This last is an invaluable source for British art and artists of the late eighteenth and early nineteenth centuries, as well as for the political, social and literary history of the time. Farington knew personally most of the leading personalities in the world of art and literature. He published *Memoirs of the Life of Sir Joshua Reynolds* in 1819.

The manuscript of the *Diary* in sixteen vellum-bound volumes was presented to George V by Lady Bathurst. It was not written for publication, but kept for reference purposes. It does, nonetheless, contain many insights and observations on contemporary events in addition to summarising Farington's own activities. Two portraits of Farington by Thomas Lawrence capture his verve and sense of curiosity during a busy and enjoyable life that was only marred by his wife's early death in 1800. Selections from the *Diary* were published in an edition by James Greig in eight volumes in 1922–28, but the publication of the complete text was undertaken by Yale University Press in fourteen volumes in 1978–84 (vols I–VI edited by Kenneth Garlick and Angus Macintyre; subsequent volumes by Kathryn Cave).

# The Royal Academy

## 55
### *After* **Johann Heinrich Ramberg (1763–1840)**
*"The Exhibition of the Royal Academy, 1787"*

Engraving by Pietro Antonio Martini
(1739–1797), 37.9 × 52.5 cm

The Greek inscription in the lower margin of this print was placed over the entrance to the Great Room in Somerset House. It reads in translation, "Let no stranger to the Muses enter". The annual exhibitions of the Royal Academy were held in the Great Room which formed part of Somerset House as redesigned by Sir William Chambers (see No. 56) and opened in 1780. The Great Room measures 16.24 m long, 13.26 m wide and 9.76 m high including the lantern. It was undoubtedly the finest exhibition space in London at that date. The Great Room is now part of the Courtauld Institute Galleries.

The print shows Reynolds (holding his ear-trumpet) accompanying George IV when Prince of Wales on the occasion of the exhibition organized in 1787. Behind, on the main wall on the same vertical axis as Reynolds and the Prince of Wales, is the President's portrait of *George IV with a servant* now in the possession of the Duke of Norfolk at Arundel Castle (fig. 11). The print also illustrates the way in which the paintings were hung at the Royal Academy in the late eighteenth century, with the full-length portraits positioned very high on the wall above the height of the doors. It was on this issue that Gainsborough broke with the Royal Academy in 1784 (see Introduction pp. 13 and No. 9).

Ramberg was from Hanover and was a pupil of Benjamin West, the second President of the Royal Academy.

## 56
### *After* Sir Joshua Reynolds
### *Sir William Chambers*
### *(1723—1796)*

Mezzotint by Valentine Green
(1739—1813), 48.5 × 38 cm; 1st state

Published by V. Green on 1 December
1780

*References*: Hamilton, p. 16

*Notes*: 1. Exhibited London 1986, no.
113.

Owing to his close connections with George III and the court, Sir William Chambers played a vital role in the foundation of the Royal Academy in 1768. The King in fact appointed Chambers as the first Treasurer of the Royal Academy and his easy access to George III caused considerable discomfiture to Reynolds who was only reluctantly accepted at court.

Chambers was born in Sweden and educated in England before embarking upon a career as a merchant. He then studied architecture in Italy (1750—55), where he possibly first met Reynolds. As an architect Chambers was essentially an eclectic embracing *chinoiserie* as well as the classical style in all its manifestations. He was interested in all aspects of design including garden design. In its own field his *Treatise in Civil Architecture* (1759) is comparable in significance with Reynolds's *Discourses*. He was appointed Architect of Works by the King in 1761. He was granted the commission for rebuilding Somerset House in 1776. It was the final triumph of his career. The Royal Academy was given space on the Strand side to the west of the vestibule.

The original portrait by Reynolds was probably painted in 1779—80.[1] In the background is the Strand front of Somerset House. Reynolds presented the portrait to the Royal Academy where it was to be hung in the Assembly Room balancing the artist's *Self-portrait* (No. 58).

## 57
## Johann Zoffany
## (1733/34–1810)
### *The Academicians of the Royal Academy*

Oil on canvas, 100.7 × 147.3 cm

Millar 1210

*Exhibitions: Johann Zoffany 1733–1810,*
National Portrait Gallery, London
1976, no. 74; London, 1986, no. 171;
Cardiff, 1990–91, no. 59; *The Artist's
Model: Its Role in British Art from Lely
to Etty,* Nottingham University Art
Gallery and The Iveagh Bequest,
Kenwood, 1991, no. 5

The painting was begun in 1771 for "a great personage", meaning George III, who as patron of the newly formed Royal Academy had an obvious interest in such a composition. He had also personally recommended Zoffany for membership. The picture was exhibited to great acclaim at the Royal Academy in 1772 and a print by Richard Earlom was published in the following year. Horace Walpole annotated his catalogue of the Royal Academy exhibition as follows: "This excellent picture was done by candlelight; he made no design for it, but clapped in the artists as they came to him, and yet all the attitudes are easy and natural, most of the likenesses strong." The composition was extended at the right by the artist by about 19.6 cm and it therefore probably ended originally on a line with the two nude models. Zoffany had to keep his ideas for the overall composition fairly fluid, since he had to incorporate new members as they were elected while the picture progressed.

Zoffany has depicted all the members of the Royal Academy excluding Gainsborough, and George and Nathaniel Dance, but including Joseph Nollekens who was elected in 1772. Gainsborough was still working in Bath during these years. It is possible, however, that the sketch of the artist's head by Zoffany in the National Portrait Gallery was made in this context. Only one artist, the Chinese modeller Tan-che-qua, was, technically speaking, not a member of the Royal Academy, but having arrived in England in 1769 happened to be in the Schools of the Royal Academy when Zoffany was working on the painting. The two female Acade-

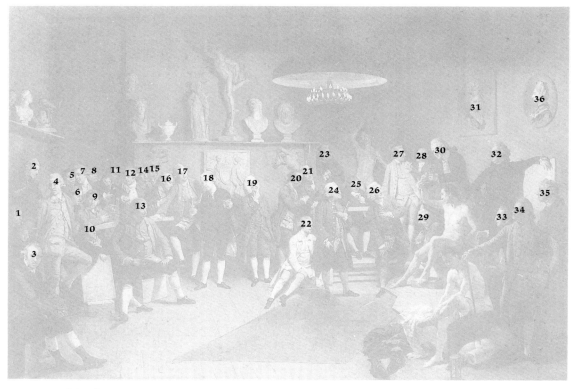

1. John Gwynn
2. Giovanni Battista Cipriani
3. Johann Zoffany
4. Benjamin West
5. Tan-che-qua
6. George Barret
7. Jeremiah Meyer
8. Dominic Serres
9. Joseph Wilton
10. Mason Chamberlin
11. Paul Sandby
12. Thomas Sandby
13. Francis Hayman
14. William Tyler
15. John Inigo Richards
16. Francis Milner Newton
17. Sir William Chambers
18. Sir Joshua Reynolds
19. William Hunter
20. Francesco Bartolozzi
21. Agostino Carlini
22. Charles Catton
23. Richard Wilson
24. Richard Yeo
25. Samuel Wale
26. Francesco Zuccarelli
27. Edward Penny
28. Peter Toms
29. Edward Burch
30. George Richard Moser
31. Angelica Kauffman
32. Nathaniel Hone
33. Joseph Nollekens
34. Richard Cosway
35. William Hoare
36. Mrs Mary Moser

micians, Mary Moser and Angelica Kauffman, are portrayed in roundels on the wall on the right for reasons of propriety as regards the nude male models. The head of Bartolozzi has been reworked and Zoffany may have made alterations to the arrangement on the shelf behind Wilson. Zoffany has recreated the scene in one of the rooms in the Royal Academy shortly after the institution had been granted permission to use rooms in Old Somerset House. Apart from drawing from the posed model, Zoffany's picture alludes to the other method of drawing, namely from casts after famous pieces of sculpture. The artist has included himself in the lower left corner holding his palette.

## 58
### *After* Sir Joshua Reynolds
### *Sir Joshua Reynolds, Doctor of Civil Law*

Mezzotint by Valentine Green, 48 × 37.7 cm; 1st state

Published by V. Green on 1 December 1780

*References*: Hamilton, p. 57

*Notes*: 1. Original painting exhibited London, 1986, no. 116. Van Dyck's *Iconography* was published posthumously in 1645 with two further editions in the seventeenth and eighteenth centuries.

The artist has depicted himself in the robes of a Doctor of Civil Law, a degree conferred on him by the University of Oxford in 1773. This self-portrait was clearly inspired by Rembrandt, although it has been established that the pose is derived from the etched portrait of Adam de Coster in Van Dyck's *Iconography*.[1] Reynolds portrays himself in the presence of a bust of Michelangelo (based on the bronze bust by Daniele da Volterra). It is a self-portrait that assumes particular significance in the context of Reynolds's final Discourse (10 December 1790), in which he took his farewell of the students of the Royal Academy. "I reflect, not without vanity, that these Discourses bear testimony of my admiration of that truly divine man; and I should desire that the last words which I should pronounce in this Academy, and from this place, might be the name of – MICHAEL ANGELO." A miniature on enamel by Henry Bone (Walker 783) dates from 1804 and shows far more vibrant colouring, which is no longer evident in the painting. The portrait was undertaken as a pair to that of Sir William Chambers (No. 56) for display in the Assembly Room of the Royal Academy in Somerset House.

## 59
### *After* **Sir Joshua Reynolds**
*Giuseppe Baretti*
*(1719—1789)*

Mezzotint by John Watts (exhibited 1766–86), 45 × 32.5 cm; 2nd state

Published by J. Boydell on 18 July 1780

*References*: Hamilton, p. 5

*Notes*: 1. Exhibited London, 1986, no. 85.

The print is based on the portrait painted for Henry Thrale and exhibited by Reynolds at the Royal Academy in 1774.[1] Baretti was born in Turin and after gaining a literary reputation in Italy arrived in London in 1751 where he became friendly with Samuel Johnson (see Nos. 25, 28). He returned to Italy in 1760, but finally settled in London at the beginning of the 1770s. His two most famous publications were *Dictionary of the English and Italian Language* (1760) and *A Journey from London to Genoa, through England, Portugal, Spain, and France* (1770). Reynolds appointed Baretti to the post of Secretary for Foreign Correspondence at the Royal Academy. In this capacity he wrote the first official guide to the Academy (1781) and translated the *Discourses* (1778) into Italian. He was tutor in Italian and Spanish to the Thrale family at Streatham Park (1773–76), where the portrait by Reynolds, like No. 25, was hung in the library. The characterization of the sitter emphasizes his short-sightedness, but this enables Reynolds to suggest the high level of his intelligence and the intensity of his scholarly pursuits.

60

**After Johann Heinrich Ramberg**

Fan: *The Royal Family viewing the Royal Academy exhibition of 1788*

Length of guardstick, 28.4 cm; guards and sticks: japanned wood with gilt and painted decoration; pin: mother-of-pearl and metal; pivot: ivory, tortoise-shell on base of guardsticks; leaf: paper recto and verso

Stipple and line engraving, hand coloured in watercolour and bodycolour; edged with gold leaf; appliqué decoration of coloured fabric flowers

The decoration on the fan is based on the print of 1788 by Pietro Antonio Martini (No. 61). However, a second print of 1790 was the immediate source for the fan, and in this the figures in the central group have been rearranged (Prince Ernest has been added on the extreme right next to Prince Edward, and two young princes – William Henry and Frederick – stand between George III and the Prince of Wales), and the figures on the right (mainly Academicians, including Reynolds) have been replaced by the figures occurring on the left of the earlier print, now seen in reverse. A second fan decorated with an impression of the same print is in the Victoria and Albert Museum and is accompanied by an engraved key.

## 61

*After* **Johann Heinrich Ramberg**

*"Portraits of Their Majesty's and the Royal Family Viewing the Exhibition of the Royal Academy, 1788"*

Engraving by Pietro Antonio Martini,
35 × 49.8 cm

The print depicts the visit of George III and Queen Charlotte with several members of their family to the annual exhibition of the Royal Academy in 1788. As in the previous year (see No. 55), Reynolds (holding his ear-trumpet) accompanies the royal party.

## 62

## *After* Sir Joshua Reynolds
## *George III*

Mezzotint by William Dickinson (1746–1823) and Thomas Watson (1750–1781), 80.5 × 50.5 cm; 1st state

Published by T. Watson and W. Dickinson on 25 April 1781

*References*: Hamilton, p. 31

Reynolds painted George III and Queen Charlotte (figs. 6, 7) in 1779 for the first exhibition held by the Royal Academy at Somerset House in 1780. The portraits were subsequently hung in the Council Room, where they can be seen in the painting *The Royal Academicians in General Assembly* by Henry Singleton (1766–1839) dating from 1795 (fig. 16). Although neither the King nor the Queen particularly liked Reynolds, it would have been impossible for George III as patron of the Royal Academy to have refused to be painted by the first President. The results, however, were far from satisfactory – stiff, dull, lifeless, with the relationship between the figures and the settings unhappily resolved.

Fig. 16 Henry Singleton, *"The Royal Academicians in General Assembly"*, 1795, oil on canvas, 198 × 259 cm, Royal Academy of Arts, London

## 63
## *After* Sir Joshua Reynolds
## *Theory*

Mezzotint by Joseph Grozer
(ca. 1755–died before 1799),
40.7 × 41.7 cm

Published by J. Grozer on 29 March
1785

*References*: Hamilton, p. 146

The print is based on the painting executed by Reynolds to decorate the coved ceiling of the Library of the Royal Academy in Somerset House, where it was surrounded by other allegorical figures (*Nature, History, Allegory, Fable*) painted by Giovanni Battista Cipriani. The painting is now installed in Burlington House. The print shows the points of a pair of dividers emanating from behind the head of the figure, but this is not evident in the painting as seen today, although the feature is confirmed by Baretti's description quoted below. A pair of dividers is often regarded as the attribute specifically of Architecture or Mathematics, but more generally it represents order, proportion, reason and judgement. Baretti (see No. 59) in his *Guide* to the Royal Academy described the composition as follows: "The Center-Painting represents the *Theory of the Art* under the form of an elegant and majestick female, seated in the clouds, and looking upwards, as contemplating the Heavens. She holds in one hand the Compass, in the other a Label, on which this sentence is written: *THEORY is the Knowledge of what is truly NATURE.*" The visual source for the figure, particularly the position of the legs and the drapery, has been identified as by Raphael, namely the angel accompanying the planet Mars in the mosaic decoration he designed for the cupola of the Chigi Chapel in Santa Maria del Popolo, Rome. The windswept appearance of the figure is in keeping with the style of several portraits by Reynolds dating from around 1780.

64

*After* **Sir Joshua Reynolds**

William Etty (1787–1849)
*Georgiana, Duchess of Devonshire (1757–1806) with her Daughter, Lucy Georgiana Cavendish (1783–1858)*

Oil on canvas, 111.8 × 148.3 cm

Millar 1041

*References*: D. Farr, *William Etty*, London, 1958, p. 182, no. 297

The original painting from which Etty made this life-size copy is one of Reynolds's most famous compositions in the Baroque style, inspired by Rubens and Van Dyck. The painting was exhibited at the Royal Academy in 1786 and shows mother and daughter playing a nursery game. It is still at Chatsworth and is a well preserved example of the artist's late style.

Georgiana was the daughter of the first Earl Spencer. She married the 5th Duke of Devonshire in 1774. Her own daughter, depicted here, married the 6th Earl of Carlisle in 1801. The Duchess of Devonshire was one of the great beauties of her age not so much because of her features but more through the force of her personality. Reynolds had also painted her as a girl with her own mother in a composition (now at Althorp) that is by contrast remarkably restrained.

George IV was on friendly terms with the Duchess of Devonshire and commissioned this copy from Sir Thomas Lawrence in 1825. In fact, Lawrence passed the commission to Etty who had worked for Lawrence at an earlier stage of his career. Interestingly, payment for the copy was made to Lawrence, but Etty himself told Richard Redgrave that he was responsible for the copy. Etty, who specialised in painting the female nude, also made a copy of Reynolds's *Cymon and Iphigenia* (see No. 14).

## 65
**Sir Joshua Reynolds**
*Cardinal Guido
Bentivoglio (1579–1644)*
(after Van Dyck)

Oil on canvas, 137.8 × 113.7 cm

Millar 1237

*Notes*: 1. E. Larsen, *The Paintings of
Anthony Van Dyck*, II, Freren 1988, no.
332. 2. British Museum
1859.5.14.305, folio 28v.

Van Dyck's portrait was painted in Rome in 1623 and entered the collection of Ferdinando II de' Medici in 1653.[1] By the eighteenth century it was
on display in the Palazzo Pitti, Florence. Reynolds was in Florence from 10
May until 4 July 1752 and spent a considerable amount of his time in the
Palazzo Pitti, as is evident from his sketchbooks. A reference in one of
Reynolds's Florentine sketchbooks in the British Museum to 'cardinal with
a bit of paper in his Hand' may refer to this portrait by Van Dyck, but it
should be noted that this folio has been pasted into the sketchbook.[2]

The attribution of this copy to Reynolds was traditional, but was rejected by Millar. It is not difficult to see why Van Dyck's portrait would have
fascinated the young Reynolds and the handling is close enough in style to
warrant a renewal of interest in the possibility that the copy is actually by
him.

## 66

**Sir Joshua Reynolds**
*Self-portrait*

Oil on panel, 75.2 × 63.2 cm

Millar 1008

*Exhibitions*: London, 1986, no. 149;
Cardiff, 1990–91, no. 41

*References*: Waterhouse, *Reynolds*, p. 85;
D. Mannings, *Sir Joshua Reynolds PRA
(1723–1792). The Self-Portraits*, Plymouth
City Museum and Art Gallery, 1992,
no. 22

*Notes*: 1. Exhibited London, 1986, no.
166.

As many as twenty-three self-portraits by Reynolds, some drawn but most
painted (or engraved after paintings), are known to have existed. The
present example, which proved to be very popular and was much copied in
a variety of media, was almost certainly painted in 1788, when the artist
was aged about sixty-five. This painted self-portrait is the penultimate of
the series. The final self-portrait (private collection) was painted at about
the same time, but shows the artist without his spectacles.

Edmond Malone, a close friend of Reynolds and his biographer (see No.
51), described this painting as "extremely like him" and "exactly as he
appeared in his latter days, in domestick life". From 1782 when the painter
suffered "a violent inflammation of the eyes", Reynolds wore silver-
rimmed spectacles for painting. He was, in fact, short-sighted. He appears
not to have worn spectacles all the time and this is the only self-portrait to
show him wearing them. The spectacles still exist in a private collection.[1]

The painting was in the possession of Reynolds's niece, Mary Palmer,
Marchioness of Thomond, who gave it to George IV in 1812 remarking
that in her opinion it was "the best portrait he ever painted of himself".
George IV had already hung enamels by Henry Bone (Walker 783–84) of
two of the artist's self-portraits (No. 59 and the present example) in his
Private Bedroom in Carlton House.

## 67

### *After* **Sir Joshua Reynolds**

Henry Bone

*Cupid and Psyche*

Signed and dated lower right: *H. Bone 1803*

Enamel, 21.2 × 26.0 cm

Walker 789

*Notes*: 1. Waterhouse, *Reynolds*, p. 81

Reynolds's original painting dates from 1789 when it was shown in the Royal Academy exhibition.[1] It is therefore comparable in date with No. 14. The source for the story of Cupid and Psyche is Apuleius, *The Golden Ass*, Books IV–VI. Reynolds depicts the moment when Psyche spies on Cupid while he is asleep. She has been expressly told not to look at Cupid, who only visited her at night. Oil drips from the lamp cause Cupid to awaken and Psyche is punished.

## 68

### *After* **Sir Joshua Reynolds**

Henry Bone

*Nymph and Cupid*

Enamel, 23.6 × 19.0 cm

Walker 795

1. Waterhouse, *Reynolds*, p. 76.

The original picture was exhibited by Reynolds at the Royal Academy in 1785, entitled *Venus*. It was bequeathed by the artist to Earl of Upper Ossory.[1]

## 69

### *After* **Sir Joshua Reynolds**

Henry Bone

*Hope nursing Love*

Signed and dated lower right: *H. Bone 1808*

Enamel, 23.4 × 18.5 cm

Walker 796

*Notes*: 1. Waterhouse, *Reynolds*, p. 60.

The original painting was exhibited at the Royal Academy in 1769 and is now at Bowood in the collection of the Earl of Shelburne.[1]

All three enamels (Nos. 67–69), like Nos. 29 and 31, were hung in George IV's Private Bedroom in Carlton House.

## Abbreviations:

### Books

Chaloner Smith
J. Chaloner Smith, *British Mezzotint Portraits . . .*, 4 vols., London 1878–83

Cormack
M. Cormack, *The Paintings of Thomas Gainsborough*, Cambridge University Press 1991

Hamilton
E. Hamilton, *A Catalogue Raisonné of the Engraved Works of Sir Joshua Reynolds PRA from 1755 to 1822 . . .*, London 1884

Millar 1963
O. Millar, *The Tudor, Stuart, and Early Georgian Pictures in the Collection of Her Majesty The Queen*, London 1963

Millar 1969
O. Millar, *The Later Georgian Pictures in the Collection of Her Majesty The Queen*, London 1969

Walker
R. Walker, *The Eighteenth and Early Nineteenth Century Miniatures in the Collection of Her Majesty The Queen*, Cambridge University Press 1992

Waterhouse, *Reynolds*
E.K. Waterhouse, *Reynolds*, London 1941

Waterhouse, *Gainsborough*
E.K. Waterhouse, *Gainsborough*, London 1958

### Exhibitions

Cardiff, 1990–91
*The Royal Collection. Paintings from Windsor Castle*, catalogue by M. Evans, National Museum of Wales, Cardiff 1990–91

London, 1980–81
*Thomas Gainsborough*, catalogue by J. Hayes, The Tate Gallery, London 1980–81

London, 1986
*Reynolds*, catalogue ed. N. Penny, Royal Academy of Arts, London 1986

Paris, 1981
*Gainsborough 1727–1788*, Grand Palais, Paris 1981

Paris, 1985
*Sir Joshua Reynolds 1729–1792*, Grand Palais, Paris, 1985

The Queen's Pictures, 1991–92
*The Queen's Pictures. Royal Collectors through the Centuries*, catalogue by C. Lloyd, National Gallery, London, 1991–92

## Selected bibliography

This list is restricted to those books that have proved to be useful for the writing of the Introduction. Nearly all of these titles have their own bibliographies.

GENERAL
*Gainsborough and Reynolds in the British Museum*, exhibition catalogue by T. Clifford, A. Griffiths and M. Royalton-Kisch, London 1978

E.K. Waterhouse, *Painting in Britain 1530–1790*, 1st edn. Harmondsworth 1953 and many subsequent editions

W.T. Whitley, *Artists and their friends in England 1700–1799*, 2 vols., London 1928

GAINSBOROUGH
M. Cormack, *The Paintings of Thomas Gainsborough*, Cambridge University Press 1991

J. Hayes, *The Drawings of Thomas Gainsborough*, 2 vols, London and New Haven 1970

J. Hayes, *Gainsborough: Paintings and Drawings*, London 1975

J. Hayes, *Thomas Gainsborough*, exhibition catalogue, The Tate Gallery, London 1980

J. Hayes, *The Landscape Paintings of Thomas Gainsborough*, 2 vols. London and Ithaca 1982

J. Lindsay, *Thomas Gainsborough. His Life and Art*, London/Toronto/Sydney/New York 1981

E.K. Waterhouse, *Gainsborough*, London 1958

W.T. Whitley, *Thomas Gainsborough*, London 1915

M. Woodall, *The Letters of Thomas Gainsborough*, 2nd edn. London 1963

REYNOLDS
D. Hudson, *Sir Joshua Reynolds. A Personal Study*, London 1958

C.R. Leslie and T. Taylor, *The Life and times of Sir Joshua Reynolds with notices of some of his Contemporaries*, 2 vols, London 1865

J. Reynolds, *The Letters*, ed. F.W. Hilles, Cambridge 1929

*Reynolds*, exhibition catalogue, ed. N. Penny, Royal Academy of Arts, London 1986

J. Reynolds, *Discourses*, ed. P. Rogers, London 1992

J. Reynolds, *Discourses on Art*, ed. R. Wark, New Haven and London 1975

E.K. Waterhouse, *Reynolds*, London 1941

THE ROYAL ACADEMY
S.C. Hutchison, *The History of The Royal Academy 1768–1986*, 2nd edn. London 1986

The help of three voluntary assistants – Alex Buck, Emma Scrase and Susannah Morris – in the preparation of the exhibition and catalogue is gratefully acknowledged.